MW01243291

Loving Emmi

How Baby Morgan The Broken Jaw Puppy
Stole Our Hearts And Our Wallet

barbara boswell brunner

with illustrations by melissa tan

edited by Katie O'Brian-Robles

ISBN: 1517621739
ISBN-13: 978-1517621735
Library Of Congress LCCN Pending

DEDICATION

For my beloved husband Ray who, without hesitation, insisted Emmi become a part of our family. His generosity, love, and tolerance for slobber are appreciated more than words can ever express.

Additionally, *Loving Emmi* is dedicated to all of the donors and supporters who so generously gave their money, gifts and time. Connie, Carol, Kevin, Flavia, Michelle, Katie, Lisa, Helen, Dotti, Debi, Dana, Linda, and countless others. We thank you from the bottom of our hearts.

CONTENTS

ACKNOWLEDGMENTS

So many people contributed to the birth of this book including editors, beta readers, family, and friends. But without Connie Shanahan, Kevin and Carol Richart of Rottie Nation Rottweiler Rescue, and a little bit of karma, we would never have had the opportunity to know Emmi's resilient, wise, and oftentimes comical spirit. Rescuing Emmi and helping her to recover from horrific injuries has been an amazing community effort. Our hearts overflow with reciprocated love. Sadly, Kevin Richart passed away before this book's completion, but I think he would be pleased with the beautiful young lady Emmi has become.

The surgeons, who operated multiple times to repair Emmi's jaw, faced a daunting task. Dr. Brett Beckman, Dr. Alexander Reiter, and Dr. Maria Soltera-Rivera, we will forever be grateful for your technical skill and generosity of spirit. Dr. Sandy Vesper, Emmi's primary veterinarian - thank you for returning my frequent middle-of-the-night texts with such patience. You all cared for Emmi as though she were your own.

Though titled *Loving Emmi*, this book also continues the journey that began in *Dog-Ma, The Zen Of Slobber* of Izzy, our feisty Parson Russell Terrier. She has faced medical challenges of her own, though not as severe as Emmi's, they are significant and important to the story.

Most of the final draft for *Loving Emmi* vanished when Izzy did the cha-cha upon the keyboard of my iPad. She somehow magically stepped on the keys in exactly the right sequence to not only delete thirty-one thousand words, but also corrupt the backup file in the Cloud - as only Izzy could do. I am quite certain my scream was heard hundreds of miles from home. My husband, Ray, and Katie O'Brian-Robles, my fellow author, friend, and editor saved the day. Working with a several day old copy, they managed to salvage and recreate most of the draft, though I am convinced that the most profound words I have ever written were deleted that day. Oh, Izzy…

PREFACE

Loving Emmi recounts the two-year saga of a tiny puppy; severely injured when she was just a few weeks of age. It is a tale of hope, inspiration, and tenacity. Some of the chapters contain graphic violence that may be upsetting to some readers. It is not intended to disturb, only to convey the complete story of how Emmi overcame her challenges and became an inspiration to so many.

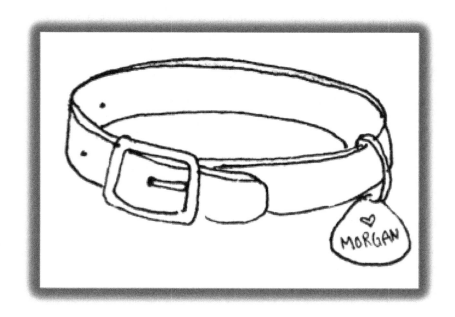

CHAPTER 1

It is said, when telling a story, to start at the beginning. For Emmi, her story begins long before she was born. Long before she became injured and ill. Long before she came into the custody of the rescue organization that saved her. Before she became the love of our lives. It begins with her namesake - Morgan.

Morgan was a beauty. A Rottweiler of enormous personality; kind, thoughtful, intelligent, and so gentle that she never fought back even when Izzy, our Parson Russell Terrier, an eighth of her size, wanted to eat her alive. She was often known to pick Izzy up by the scruff of the neck, find the closest human, and drop Izzy gently at their feet, as though to say "You deal with it."

Morgan was the gentlest of giants. She was a typical Rottweiler clown. Her goal in life was to please her humans. She garnered pleasure from her ability to make people laugh. From her silly expressions to her howling accompaniment to emergency vehicle sirens, Morgan never failed to add humor to our lives.

We lost Morgan in October 2013 to cancer. We had so little warning. Only a week passed from the day she let us know she was not feeling well to the day she passed away.

Our first warning was the quiet whimper as she lay in her bed. I thought she was hungry. Morgan was never one to pass up her groceries. Exuberant eating was an Olympic-style sport for her and she finished her breakfast as she normally did, with one fast gulp. While walking her for morning bathroom duties, I noted she was straining slightly to urinate and made a mental note to watch for it later in the day. She returned indoors plopping directly onto her bed. That was unusual. Morgan was always under foot, never far from wherever we were. But that particular morning she wanted to go back to sleep in the solitude and darkness of the bedroom. I noticed as she slept, she whimpered in her dreams. It caught my attention. It was unusual behavior. By dinnertime she was not hungry and refused to eat. Not even a piece of steak would tempt her.

It happened that fast.

By morning she was passing golf-ball-sized chunks of clotted blood. Our regular vet was out of town; her back up partner was on vacation as well. A substitute vet, who appeared all of twelve years old, examined Morgan. I am sure she was in her late twenties or early thirties, but everyone looked like a baby to me after I had passed the age of forty. Her veterinary skills did not make a positive impression. After a urine culture test she stated that Morgan had a UTI. "Just a urinary tract infection. She'll be fine in 24 hours."

She prescribed antibiotics and sent us home. By mid-day, Morgan was crying in agony. This girl had been stoic her entire life. Before the age of two, she endured four major leg operations in succession with nary a complaint. One of those surgeries was to repair a broken leg, caused by a torn cranial cruciate ligament or CCL. She never cried once - before, during, or throughout the extensive recovery period. When hurting, Morgan became pensive and quiet, never expressing pain vocally. We knew that whatever was causing her to cry out was serious.

We called the substitute vet again, who sent us to get an X-ray. In hindsight, I am not sure what an X-ray would have shown since a UTI and bladder issue wouldn't show up in that type of test, but we went anyway. This childlike vet proclaimed there was nothing wrong with Morgan; she was just being a baby. Those were her exact words. She gave us some pain medication and sent us home.

I do not know where this doctor received her veterinary degree, but I suspect she was last in her class. I was angry. Mad that our regular vet, whom we loved and trusted, was out of town. Frustrated that her business partner was gone as well and that they left us in the hands of a moron. We became enraged when we later learned of the true cause of

Morgan's pain. We could have alleviated her agony much sooner, had we known.

We spent the next few days taking turns sitting near Morgan during the day and sleeping beside her at night. The pain medication helped her to sleep and we hoped it gave her relief. It allowed us to spend a few more precious days with her, giving us enough time to prepare our good-byes and for her to let us know she was ready to rest. Her eyes said it all. The love expressed in her face told us that it was ok to let her go.

Morgan was patient number one on the day of Dr. Cindy's return. She was urinating clumps of blood. We knew in our hearts it was grave. Dr. Cindy palpated Morgan's belly and discussed the fluid buildup she felt. After a thorough examination she determined Morgan was in the end stage of renal failure.

We allowed Morgan to pass with dignity, in as little pain as possible. My husband, Ray, and I are true believers in euthanasia for our beloved pets. We want them to live the best life they can. As long as they are happy, with a good quality of life, we will treat their ailments to the best of our ability. We will never extend a life to satisfy our own need for companionship. To us, it is the hardest but the greatest act of love we can show our adored animals.

With Morgan, it was just that. Kind. It was what she deserved. Putting her through surgery or complex treatments would have extended her life, but to what end? She would have lived her remaining months in pain and without dignity. Our pets are an extension of our family. If Morgan could have been the recipient of a kidney transplant we would have found a way to make it happen - if it would have provided her with more healthy years of life. But that was not an option. Morgan was simply too sick. We let her go peacefully, in the gentlest way we knew.

Dr. Cindy immediately performed a necropsy - an autopsy for animals - on Morgan's body. We all desperately needed answers. What had been missed in her most recent check-up, where she appeared to be the picture of health? Her blood work and other tests were right in line with those of a healthy dog. Dr. Cindy was as puzzled as we were. What could have been overlooked that was so severe it lead to renal failure?

A year earlier, Morgan had a bout with uveitis. An eye infection. We took her to Izzy's ophthalmologist whom we knew and trusted. She treated the uveitis, which cleared up quickly, but warned us, "When a healthy Rottweiler gets uveitis, it almost always means there is cancer lurking somewhere in the body. It is something unique to the breed." We were stunned. Morgan seemed so bright and healthy, but the ophthalmologist strongly suggested we get her to a cancer specialist for a complete check up.

Having previously lost several dogs to cancer, we felt like we knew the drill and immediately scheduled her with a recommended canine oncologist. Dr. Heidi squeezed in an appointment for Morgan the following day to do a full body ultrasound and exam. She agreed that in a Rottweiler, uveitis was a sign of cancer. After a four-hour exam and a thorough round of tests, she could find nothing. NOTHING. She told us to watch Morgan for any signs of changed behavior, but in her opinion Morgan was one of the few Rottweilers that developed uveitis without an underlying cancer component.

We breathed a sigh of relief. The eye infection healed and Morgan went back to her normal self, trying to stay one step ahead of Izzy the terrorist. Though Morgan was a senior-aged dog, she never slowed down. She made daily visits to the nursing home where Ray's mother received her round-the-clock care. Morgan loved her grandma and relished the attention from the nursing staff, other patients, and their visitors. She had a dog-buddy named Rambo who she played with daily. When weather permitted she would run around the enclosed courtyard sneaking peeks into the windows of staff and patient rooms. You could see the joy on her face when someone looked out and laughed at her. She would snuffle - a combination snort, headshake, and happy-bark then look back to Ray for approval. The care facility was directly under the flight path of a local airport. This is where she did her best and most acrobatic airplane chasing - up and down the grassy area, ears flapping, and feet rarely touching the ground. Morgan had well honed entertainment skills. Her goal in life was to bring joy to her humans. When she made the grumpiest person laugh, her work was accomplished. There was always a twinkle in her eye.

Flash forward to the necropsy procedure. Dr. Cindy called a few hours later. Veterinarians are generally quite stoic, having daily interaction with illness and death. A hard protective shell to guard their emotions must be a necessity. Her voice cracked as she told me the results. When she opened up Morgan she found CANCER – bi-lateral renal cancer. It was so advanced that it had fused her kidneys together. Dr. Cindy was stunned. I have the necropsy photographs that were taken that day and still cannot look at them. I hold onto them as a reminder of how quickly cancer can take our loved ones: humans or four-legged friends.

Morgan never made us aware of her pain. Over the course of the year following the bout with uveitis, the only medical issue she had was occasional bladder leakage. We treated her for spay incontinence, which is a common affliction in aging, spayed, female dogs. She played normally, she went on as many long walks as her super-bionic legs could handle, and sunned herself beside the pool every afternoon. The ophthalmologist who diagnosed the uveitis and predicted cancer, later said that the cancer cells were probably in their infancy; not yet even detectable when we sought help from the oncologist.

The unexpected loss of Morgan left us with a palpable sadness. I was mad at the world. Angry that cancer existed, angry that we had so little time to prepare for the loss. Within a two-year span we had lost our dogs Madison and Cooper. We also lost Ray's mom to Alzheimer's. Now it was Morgan. Little did we know that in a few short months we would also lose my father and my sister. I like to think of them all together at the Rainbow Bridge, happy, healthy, and watching over us.

My dear friend, Katie O'Brian-Robles, author of *Life With A*

DoberDiva, wrote me this lovely letter after Morgan's passing, using Morgan's voice. She selected several quirky behaviors of the dogs included in *Dog-Ma, The Zen Of Slobber,* building them into Morgan's letter. It was a thoughtful gesture that brought us great comfort.

Hi Mom.

It's me. Morgan. Or "Saint Morgan" as they call me here. Thank you so much for letting me come to Heaven. I can't tell you how beautiful it is. The rolling hills go on for miles and miles and are covered with the greenest, softest, most sweet smelling grass.

Guess what Mom? I can run now. I can run like the wind I can. Just yesterday Cooper and I had a race (Did I tell you Cooper is here too??) He still loves butter and lines little pats of it all in a straight line, just for fun. But I'm getting ahead of myself. Cooper and I had a race and beat those silly gazelles with the crinkly horns – left them in the dust we did.

Oh, oh, oh, before I forget, Lexington says to tell you hello and to let you know that he can see you and misses you, but he is so happy here too. We're together and watch you all of the time. Try not to be sad. Please be brave for all of us. You taught us that, you know. We get sad when we see you sad, and you are so much prettier when you flash that 500-watt smile....there...that's better.

We're right beside you. All you have to do is reach out and scratch us behind our ears like you used to do. We feel it, honest we do. Especially Turbo with those glorious Spock ears of his!! Always the adventurer; he's taking surfing lessons from Kashi. He "foofs' his way all the way to the shore. Kashi has her own private beach and only invites Gus and Sutton. (Madison can't come. Not until she gives St. Peter back his halo. Yep... she's still a thief!)

Lexington is usually too busy playing golf. He doesn't use the golf carts though... he likes to walk the course.

When I first got here, I was a little confused. I felt something growing out of my shoulders... wasn't sure what they were. Sutton came over (she's so brave now,) and told me they were wings. Beautiful white feathery wings. Mom. God has given me WINGS! I'm the only dog in Heaven with them. I'm an 'angel dog' now. I can run AND fly and watch over all the creatures that are so happily scampering, hopping, galloping, slithering, and napping here. All except cats... there are no cats in Heaven... but we always knew that didn't we.

I love you Mom. You gave me such a wonderful life. You and Dad were so kind and loving. I ate the best food, and got the most delicious baths. (I just pretended not to like them.) I slept the best sleep and had the best dreams, and guess what? My dreams came true. It's exactly what I imagined.

Tell Izzy that when she gets here she will see the most amazing colors, and she'll be able to swim like a little fish and give Madison lessons... that is IF she'll return all the things the little klepto has stolen. I think she's just being her extra friendly self and wants the owners to come to her house and play. Ooorrr... maybe not. She's gotten to be quite the collector.

Gotta go.... Gus ran off looking for ducks, and I want to help Sutton find McDonald's; they have a burger waiting... Without pickles. We'll see you soon, (time flies when you're in Heaven.)

Love, Morgan

Though taken from us entirely too soon, Morgan lived a wonderful life. She was born in Oregon, living with us in both California and Florida. She had multiple canine brothers and sisters whom she adored. Madison and Gus were the elders, taught her the ropes; making every possible attempt to keep her out of trouble when she was young. She was the one dog we can truly say never did a single bad thing when she was small. Not one. She had so many playmates with good common sense that it kept her safe. Cooper was her best buddy and shadow. He and our second Rottweiler, Sutton, had been inseparable. As Sutton faded from a yearlong battle with spinal cancer, Cooper lost his playmate.

Cooper was an extremely sensitive and empathetic soul. He was unsure of Morgan on the day we brought her home. Not much time had passed since the loss of Sutton and we weren't sure if his heart was ready to accept another furry friend. Morgan was just a tiny twelve-pound fluff-ball, but he was terrified of her. (Cooper missed "Bravery Training Day" when he was learning how to be a Doberman.) However, he quickly realized she was exactly like one of his treasured plush toys except she also played back. They quickly became great companions chasing each other up and down the hills behind our Oregon home. As Morgan matured, synchronized sleeping was their favorite sport.

Then Izzy entered our lives. Our little holy terror. From the minute we brought her home she was a constant behavioral challenge but Cooper adored her instantly. The two of them had an indescribable bond. He never let Izzy out of his sight, kept her safe, and tried his best to keep her out of trouble. He would push her around with his long Doberman noodle-nose. Cooper was an unusually tall Doberman and Izzy was just seven pounds on the day we brought her home. She didn't even reach his knees but Cooper never injured her once. He was as gentle as a doting mother, yet a confident disciplinarian.

We never did understand why Morgan and Izzy began fighting. Or to clarify - why Izzy tried to fight with Morgan. It was, in all likelihood, Izzy wanting desperately to be the Alpha dog after Cooper died. In her head she was much larger than her actual size and quite entitled to authority. Izzy was bestowed the nickname "policewoman" for obvious reasons. I think she would have been quite pleased with a badge and gun, as well. She wanted to be the enforcer of all rules - except the rules SHE was supposed to obey. When Izzy did not want to respect the house rules, she developed Sudden-Onset-Convenient-Deafness.

Morgan generally scoffed at her. Their battles were one sided, but often turned bloody, most often because Izzy had self-inflicted wounds. When a small terrier head bounces around inside the mouth of a one-hundred-plus pound Rottweiler, there's bound to be damage. Izzy had to wear a muzzle anytime the two of them were together. The irony never failed to make us laugh. It was the cute, fuzzy terrier in the Hannibal Lecter mask not the big scary-looking Rottweiler. Her muzzle was a pretty pink leather contraption with silver sparkly flowers decorating it, fitted so that she could drink comfortably. At some point we had to add a head strap, from snout to neck, to prevent the little stinker from pulling it off. Izzy had always been devilishly clever. It became known as her "suicide prevention device." As long as Izzy was muzzled we had peace and Morgan could nap in relaxed comfort. Izzy would still jump on Morgan's head occasionally, startling her from a sound sleep, but as long as Morgan didn't get bitten she did her best to ignore Izzy. She was so tolerant.

In the weeks following Morgan's passing, we kept busy. With a book tour in progress for my first book, *Dog-Ma, The Zen Of Slobber*, we loaded Izzy in the car with us and commenced on a road trip. We had an event scheduled in Northern Florida with the Leon County Humane Society, a no-kill shelter, who depended solely on community fundraising for support.

The event began at dusk in a beautifully converted dairy farm property. Strings of twinkling lights hung in hundred-year-old oak trees, illuminating the lawn. A lively country music band played in the barn, where, later, an auction would be held to raise money for the shelter. The coordinator set us up at a high-top table where Ray, Izzy, and I signed hundreds of books; all purchased by a private donor and given as a part of the attendee swag bag. Each recipient wanted his or her book personalized and autographed. It was a lot of inscriptions and signature artistry for one night. My fingers were cramped and tired, but we had so much fun interacting with all of the dog-lovers in attendance. Many had heartwarming stories to share of their own animals.

Izzy admirers asked for a "pawtograph" - an ink stamp of Izzy's footprint. It was a frequent request at book signing events. Izzy's allergies were so severe, in order to save her paws from an allergic reaction to ink, we had a paw print stamp made from her actual footprint.

One of Izzy's many nicknames was "Bubble Dog," a reference to her severe allergies. The name derivation is from a 1992 Seinfeld television episode titled "Bubble Boy," where a young boy is placed in a germ-free plastic "bubble" to protect him from infection and allergies. Izzy's life would be much less complicated if she were placed into a hermetically sealed enclosure. Her allergy triggers include almost all foods, airborne pollens, and contact allergens. Izzy's kibble was specially formulated from the protein of chicken feather quills combined with vitamins and minerals. It gave her all of the nutrition she needed to stay alive. Initially we placed Izzy on this food as a temporary measure, but as we reintroduced her to normal food, she became anaphylactic. Her face swelled like a blowfish. We took no chances with her and a good supply of Benadryl and an Epi Pen were never far from reach. Many fans would offer her treats at book signing events and it sometimes took a Herculean leap over the table to intervene.

Throughout the evening's events, I signed books, Ray stamped Izzy's footprint alongside my signature, and Izzy got hugs and kisses. And a few photo-ops. Izzy loved the attention and she had no shortage of fans. During the course of the event, many sweet shelter dogs were paraded through the well-heeled crowd with high hopes of finding them forever homes. We had many attendees ask if Izzy was also available for adoption. Everyone wanted to take her home. One of the event coordinators brought Izzy a pretty, handmade flower ornament for her collar that said "I've Been Adopted" so people would stop asking. Izzy, of course, loved the flower ornament so much that she ate it.

An exasperated utterance of "Oh Izzy" was such a common phrase for us to mutter to our little devil-dog, whom we loved and adored... with our whole hearts... really... We often shared stories with other terrier owners and we all had one common thought. The only reason the Russell Terrier breed survived was because they were so darn cute. We once asked the owner of a fifteen year old Parson Russell Terrier when hers started to calm down. Her answer was "I'll let you know when it happens. So far, it hasn't..."

At the end of the evening, the event coordinator presented both Ray and I with a gift, thanking us for our time. Cynthia Rylant's book, *Dog Heaven*, was signed by every person employed at the Leon County Humane Society. They wrote beautiful messages of compassion for our loss of Morgan. We wept at their thoughtfulness and kind gesture. My favorite inscription was this:

> *"Barbara and Ray, We wanted to give you this book to honor Morgan and the seven pack members that went before her. Each new pet never replaces an old one, it just expands our hearts. Thank you for opening up your hearts to so many deserving dogs. Your book lets us share in the joy of their lives and weep with their loss. May your memories comfort you until you meet again – which I know you will." -Tracy*

CHAPTER 2

Book signings were fun for us to do as a family. Izzy loved the attention and book lovers always enjoyed meeting one of the stars of *Dog-Ma, The Zen Of Slobber*. Izzy would often lie beside a pile of books, right up on the table, to watch the crowd. She was my circus barker, drawing people over to see what in the heck a cute little dog was doing sitting on the table. She was a wonderful assistant.

Once home from our two-week book tour, Morgan's absence was panoptic. We gathered her bed and toys, donating them to our local animal shelter in hopes that it would help us to close the Morgan-chapter of our lives. A few special items were given to friends. It didn't help. We had not lived in a single-dog home for decades and surprisingly Izzy was lonely too. When we adopted Izzy we had four other dogs in our home. Gus; a Brittany, Madison; a Dalmatian/Black Lab, Cooper, and Morgan. All were rescues. All were large. Gus was the smallest at fifty pounds and Morgan was the largest at one hundred and sixty-five. Izzy was accustomed to having a lot of canine companions.

We started the hunt for a dog to add to our family. With Izzy's track record for feistiness, we had some fairly specific parameters. Her best friend had been Cooper. From the day we brought her home, they were inseparable. He was her protector, her guide, and her disciplinarian. He adored her and she idolized him. Izzy witnessed the tragic event that cost Cooper his life. It scarred her forever.

Cooper had survived nine years of life with Von Willebrands Deficiency or vWD. It is a genetic bleeding disorder similar to hemophilia in humans and common in many breeds including Dobermans. vWD dogs lack blood-clotting factor. If even slightly injured he stood a chance of bleeding to death. No matter where we lived, we alerted every neighbor to his condition. They were generally zealous in their assistance and helped keep Cooper safe.

After living in Florida for some time, a new family purchased the home next door to us. The man of the house did not like dogs and especially did not like Cooper, who reciprocated with his own vocally demonstrative dislike. Cooper had always been a great judge of character and he took pride in protecting his family from those he deemed not worthy. He rarely barked unless he was alerting us to danger and with this new neighbor, his barking was often heard through the neighborhood. Other neighbors commented to us that Cooper's new barking habit was odd. They had all known him for years and knew it was out of the ordinary. He possessed a quiet and introverted personality.

The new neighbor's complaints were so frequent that we purchased a citronella bark-deterrent collar for Cooper just a week prior to his death. We hated using it, but wanted to appease the complaints. When we apologized to the neighbor, telling him we purchased the collar, his response was "too little, too late." We were puzzled by the aggressive response to our sincere apology.

On the day of the event that took Cooper's life, I was working in our kitchen where the dog door to the yard was located. Cooper and Izzy had gone outside to explore in our fenced dog yard. Cooper's sudden barking was rapid and ferocious. Out of character for him. Then as quickly as it started, the barking ceased being replaced by a blood-curdling yelp. Cooper and Izzy came crashing through the dog door at high speed. Cooper was crying, shaking and Izzy appeared terrified. I immediately sprinted outside to investigate, finding the neighbor and his friend working with hand tools alongside our fence. I asked what had occurred. Neither looked up from their work but replied "nothing." They had to have heard him cry; he was merely a few feet away from where they were crouched on the ground. I commented that I heard Cooper cry out before he came bounding into the house. Again, their response was a mumbled denial that they had seen or heard anything out of the ordinary. I was perplexed.

Later that evening Cooper began limping. By midnight he was unable to walk. The following afternoon he was dead. Because he showed no outward signs of illness, necropsy was performed revealing he had received a blow to the spine with a hard round object about the size of a hammerhead. He bled to death, slowly, and right before our eyes. Izzy was so terrified of what happened to Cooper that she never again used the dog door or yard, even if we accompanied her.

The neighbor was a doctor. As a medical professional, he and his wife understood the gravity of Cooper's Von Willebrand's Deficiency. We discussed it at length with them shortly after they moved in. There is no excuse to ever hit an animal, especially one with this condition. We can only speculate what happened since Izzy has no vocal communication skills. For years we watched her body language with this neighbor and she never forgot nor forgave what happened to her best friend.

In our quest to find Izzy a new companion, we were comfortable searching for a male Doberman and wanted a rescue. The tricky part was getting a puppy or young dog so that Izzy could retain her imaginary status as leader of the pack. We had to keep up the illusion that she was somehow in charge of the household. If you have ever owned or known a Russell Terrier, you will completely understand. They are big dogs in little bodies - feisty, demanding, and confidant. A bit Napoleonic.

Finding puppies in a rescue situation is rare and when they are available they can suffer from poor breeding and health issues. We needed to be cautious and do our research. Izzy would most likely live for many more years and we wanted a companion for her that was healthy.

Our Doberman search had begun. The Facebook dog rescue family is large, spreading throughout the world. It seemed like a logical place to commence. A month went by and many dog biographies crossed my Facebook Page, but none were the right fit. Some were older and set in their ways or they had illnesses we didn't feel equipped to care for. Some were best suited to be an only-dog with just humans as companions. Some simply didn't move us.

Then I fell in love. A young red Doberman, named Cinnabar, popped up on a breed-specific rescue site in Canada. He looked perfect. Young, but not a puppy, good with small dogs and there was something about his face. Most Dobermans are very intelligent and possess expressive faces. Red-coated Dobermans seem to be additionally more intuitive and silly. Cinnabar's kind soul radiated from his face and grabbed my heart in an instant. I was captivated and immediately sent in an application. I wrote a novel-length commentary, knowing how difficult it would be to convince a rescue located two thousand miles away to trust a total stranger with one of their dogs. I asked a few mutual connections to vouch for my husband and me and our commitment to the dogs in our life.

Sadly, we were quickly turned down. The director of the rescue felt it was too risky to transport a dog that far. What if he didn't work out? We might just abandon Cinnabar in a Florida shelter. I certainly understood the logic, but was still heartbroken. Did the director not know WHOM he was dealing with? The self-proclaimed dog addict? I could no more take a dog to a shelter than I could cut off my own arm. Seriously! We accept the hand we are dealt with the dogs we have chosen to bring into our family. Good grief, Izzy still had a home. She's a dog that any other family might have abandoned years ago with her temperament, health, and behavioral issues. But we loved her despite the daily challenges she presented. Cinnabar remained in the Canadian rescue for months but did eventually find the perfect home. I still check in on him from time to time. And amusingly, Cinnabar's photo appears as one of the most commented upon photos in my Facebook generated movie from 2014.

We continued our Doberman search but focused it closer to home. A tiny unnamed male puppy came into a North Carolina rescue on a Saturday afternoon. Ray and I were not completely convinced we could handle a puppy anymore, but we applied despite our reservations. A puppy brought with it a whole host of things that would make us lose sleep for a while, but if Izzy would be happy, it would be worth the sleep deprivation. By Monday morning, when the weekend's applications were processed, the little guy had already found a forever home. Good for him, a letdown for us. My disappointment built into frustration. We were not going to buy a dog knowing how many are euthanized in shelters every day. We had to help one of them find its way into our home. I made a plea to a Facebook friend who is a pilot and transports rescue dogs throughout the East Coast of the United States. I asked him to please be on the lookout for a puppy or young male Doberman. He said he would, and posted the request to his Facebook Page.

Literally, within five minutes, his post got a response in which I was tagged.

CONNIE: Hi Barbara Boswell Brunner. I know it is not a Doberman, but I am on my way to pick up a puppy right now and our rescue could sure use your help as a foster parent while you wait to find your puppy.

BARBARA: What kind of puppy is it? Why is it coming into rescue? Male or Female?

CONNIE: It's a female Rottweiler. Eight weeks old. We were told it has some sort of birth defect and its mouth will not open. I won't know more until I pick it up.

BARBARA: I don't know how our current dog will do with another female Rottweiler. She has "history" but we can certainly help you out for a couple of days.

CONNIE: Great. I will call you when I know more.

As it turned out, Connie lived in the same neighborhood, just a few streets away from us. We belonged to many of the same dog rescue and transport groups, yet had never met. She was getting less active with rescue and was only picking up this puppy because no one else was available on such short notice. Karma? Kismet? Somehow our connection was meant to be. In the years following our initial meeting, Connie and her husband Jim became dear friends.

Connie picked up the emaciated, flea covered puppy, and rushed it to her personal veterinarian for an examination. The story told to Connie when the puppy was surrendered was that the puppy's canine mother had bitten it in the head when it tried to eat from her food bowl. The veterinarian confirmed that the puppy had damage to her jaw, not a birth defect. It most likely had sustained a broken jaw from the mother's bite but more tests would need to be done to confirm the suspicion. In fairness to the puppy's mother, Rottweilers are notoriously poor mothers. Not because they lack maternal instincts, but because they are clumsy and huge. Injuries among puppies in large breeds are not uncommon. The breeder should have done a better job of supervision.

The breeder signed the puppy over to the rescue, relinquishing all rights to it. Connie contacted me to discuss the veterinarian visit and to let me know she had taken the puppy to Carol, the Director of Rottie Nation Rottweiler Rescue, for more extensive testing. The puppy would need to stay at the rescue facility until testing was completed. Later that evening a post was made on the rescue's Facebook Page announcing that this little pup needed a very expensive MRI. "What to do?" still resonates in my head. We were so worried they would choose to euthanize because of the cost of an MRI. Rottie Nation Rottweiler Rescue was a brand new rescue group whose coffers had not yet built up a surplus to handle this unexpected high-level cost.

Ray and I talked it over and together decided if the rescue was unable to cover the cost of the MRI, then we would personally pay for it. The puppy deserved a chance. A call was placed to Carol the next morning and arrangements were made with our personal veterinarian to see the puppy later that day. We would take on the responsibility of becoming this puppy's medical foster home; arrange her veterinarian appointments, transport her as needed and most importantly, fundraise to help pay her bills. The path we were headed down was not apparent to us that day. We honestly thought the extent of our involvement would be an MRI and possibly a surgery to correct whatever problem was discovered. Once healed, we would hand the little fur-ball off to her new family. That was how fostering animals was supposed to work. Hahaha! We were so naïve.

Ray and I drove an hour to meet Carol and pick up the puppy. We met in the parking lot of a shopping mall halfway between our home and the rescue, since traveling to the actual rescue facility was cumbersome. Carol filled our car with food and toys before introducing us to our new little furry charge. We had paperwork to sign, plans to coordinate, and finances to discuss. The puppy stayed in the air-conditioned car for some time.

Finally, as she handed her over, Carol said, "Here she is. Meet your new foster pup. Her name is MORGAN."

Tears welled up in my eyes. How in the world did this sweet puppy get that name? Surely Carol had researched my Facebook Page, read about us losing OUR Morgan, and was tugging on our heartstrings. "That wasn't fair," I thought to myself. The wound of losing our Morgan was still so fresh. We would take care of this puppy no matter what. Looking at Carol's face told me she had no idea why I was so emotional. Ray jumped in to the conversation and asked how she came by that name; it was certainly an unusual name for a dog. Carol said she wasn't sure but when Connie picked her up, it is the name she put on the relinquishment paperwork after the breeder had signed her over to the rescue. Carol had no idea of the history or of our recent loss. Nor did Connie. It still gives me chills.

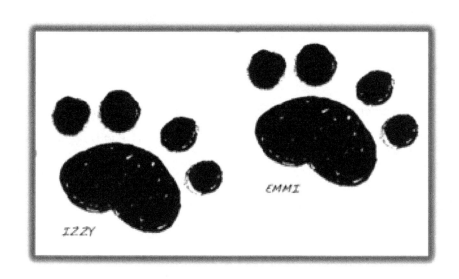

CHAPTER 3

Izzy's Perspective

Holy terrier. Mom and Dad said we were all going for a drive to pick up a surprise for me. Yay! I like surprises. I was thinking ice cream or toys. Not fur-ball. And it smells like poop. Hey, the princess does not sit with a smelly poop puppy. OK. It doesn't smell like poop. I made that up. If I don't look at it, maybe it will go away. I'll just look out the window for a while. La, la, la...

But it is kind of cute. If you like that sort of thing. I'll just sneak a peek. It's really little. I wonder why it's hiding under the pillow.

If I just stick my nose between the crate bars, maybe I can see it better.

If I push that pillow with my foot... just a little more... I can almost touch it.

HEY! It licked my nose. That tickles.

I wonder what it tastes like. Probably poop. It smells like poop. Oh, wait. No it doesn't. It tastes like... oh, I remember that stuff. Puppy breath. It's just a baby.

A quiet utterance from the front seat "Izzy, be nice."

Like I wouldn't be nice. Seriously. I'm always nice. I'm the princess. Let me just stretch my foot a little further... I won't bop it too hard... I wonder if it squeaks...

Why are mom and dad whispering about Morgan? She went away a few months ago and didn't come back. I didn't like her much. But I miss her anyway. I think she left because I was mean. I miss my brother Cooper. I wasn't mean to him. He was my buddy. There they go, talking about Morgan again.

Hey! Wait a tiny minute! Mom just reached into the fur-ball's crate and called her Morgan. Holy terrier. Did they shrink Morgan down in size? Uh oh. Maybe THAT'S why she was gone so long? Now Dad says that they better not call her that. How about just call her "M" until they think of something better. Ok. Ok. Maybe it's not Morgan.

I'm safe, but it sure does look like a miniature Morgan.

She's so little. Maybe if I just put my head down right here... next to her crate... I can keep her company. Wait. Mom just turned around and looked at me. I can't let her know I am being nice. But I'm so sleepy. I'm going to close my eyes for a minute and snuggle my head against the crate... I think the fur-ball likes me...

Emmi's Perspective

My head hurts. It's been like this for what seems like my whole life. I don't feel well. My stomach hurts too. I'm really hungry. I've tried to eat. Food smells so good, but I can't open my mouth. I don't remember the last time I could. Why can other dogs eat and I can't? I don't understand.

Every day I get handed off to some new human. They are all really nice and try to feed me. But I'm still HUNGRY! I saw a doctor yesterday that poked me with a thing he called a needle. Ouch. It hurt. Then he gave me a bath in something to get rid of the things that were biting me all over. It felt so good. The nice lady last night tried to help me eat some food.

Now I'm in another car, with another human and another dog. I'm just going to stick my head under this pillow and shut out the world. I don't feel good. The doctor said I have an infection. The darkness makes my head feel better.

The humans in the front seat seem to know the white dog. They call her Izzy and keep telling her to be nice.

I hope she's nice to me. My dog-mom wasn't very nice to me. I'm going to try very hard to be nice to that white dog. She looks like fun, but my head hurts. I can't think about fun right now. I wonder if these humans have food. I hope so. I like food. I'm hungry.

The Izzy dog won't look at me. She's sitting in her bed looking out the window. If I shuffle under this pillow, maybe she will come a little closer. Yep. That worked. Come on Izzy dog. Come say hi. I'm really nice. You stuck your nose in my crate! Here's a kiss. We're going to be good friends.

CHAPTER 4

Oh, she was so tiny. She couldn't open her mouth and hadn't eaten much for days. We later discovered she weighed only twelve pounds. We also read through the paperwork Carol had put together for us and realized she was not eight weeks old, as Connie had been told, but she was really ten weeks old. She was so malnourished that the first surgeon who operated on her told us she was just days away from death - forty percent underweight. Her blood work was terrible; none of the values put her in the range for surgery to be performed safely. She had a raging infection that should have been treated weeks earlier. The aftereffects of that infection would

in her car and drove to his home to help - in the middle of the night. So many comments were made that night on the group's Facebook Page, that it became a Trending Topic.

A simple request for help with an $800 MRI bill rapidly ballooned into medical costs exceeding $35,000. With the help of some very generous donors, an auction held by Misfit The Blind Dog (the Facebook phenomenon), and a yard sale sponsored by a local exotic bird rescue, we put a major dent in that bill. The remainder of the bills are another story. Suffice it to say our retirement fund is a bit lighter these days.

We were warned. We knew her medical needs could financially skyrocket. We were repeatedly advised it might be better to euthanize her before we became too attached. One surgeon, on a consult early in her care, told us point blank that he would euthanize her. He told us that she would never live to be six months old and would starve to death before then. An exercise in futility, he said. Another surgeon told us that we might spend $20,000 or $25,000 and still have to euthanize her. We knew the rescue could not afford her care. It would be unfair to ask when there were so many other dogs that needed their time, money, and energy. If this puppy was to survive it was going to have to be a community effort. Her virtual family would be her salvation.

Day one of our life with Baby Morgan started with a huge dilemma - her name.

Izzy's history with our Morgan disallowed any reference to that name for THIS little fur-ball. We needed to give them a chance at being friends. It would also be too uncomfortable for us. We lost Original Morgan, as we started calling her, just a few months prior. We had no intention of keeping this puppy, only fostering her through her immediate medical needs. Her eventual adopters might love the name Morgan and want to keep it. Her Facebook Page and fundraising page had already been established under the name Baby Morgan. Her medical records were already being built up under the name Morgan. We knew this could become very complicated.

The breeder named her "Precious." In the rescue world it is customary to assign each animal a new name when completing the animal-surrender paperwork. It helped to ensure the animal's anonymity once placed into a foster home. Connie needed a name for the new puppy and thought back to the first home-visit she had made for a rescue-dog placement. The family had a beautiful, dark haired, two year old daughter that had captured Connie's heart. This tiny soul, who instantly bonded to the "test dog" Connie had brought with her, was named Morgan. Connie wanted to give Precious a new name that would signify strength and kindness. She chose the name Morgan. I didn't know Connie well at this point and certainly did not want to offend her, knowing she is the one who had selected the name, so Morgan stuck.

We were not going to be her forever family anyway...

It was only going to be a few weeks...

To solve the immediate name dilemma, we began calling her "M." "M" morphed into Emmi, and the name fit her to a tee. She is Emerson when she is in BIG trouble and Ems when we need a shortcut. In her silly times Ray calls her Emmi Lou Who Dunnit. It is the one issue that confuses folks the most on her Facebook Page. Ray and I float between names for her without even thinking anymore. As she has grown older she looks and acts so much like Original Morgan that we often call her Morgan without thinking and then laugh as we catch the other in the error.

They even had similar unusual mannerisms. Original Morgan liked to chase airplanes as they flew at 35,000 feet over our home. It was hilarious, as she would bounce back and forth in the yard or on the patio with her ears flapping, barking into the sky. We'd never before had a dog with this quirk, but Emmi chased planes too. The week we brought Emmi home from her first surgery, our eyes welled with tears as we watched her snuggle into Original Morgan's favorite spot on the patio sofa. I am sure it smelled of Morgan and perhaps gave Emmi comfort. As she grew, Emmi continued to claim that spot as hers. We would often get a catch in our throat when walking by the patio doors seeing her with one paw delicately hanging over the cushion's edge, just as Morgan's had.

CHAPTER 5

Emmi's first surgery was scheduled immediately at a veterinary specialty clinic in Southwest Florida with a young, energetic and talented surgeon. He had a daunting task. Emmi was malnourished with a raging infection. Her jaw was locked shut. Just the process of intubating her for surgery allowing her to breathe was difficult. There was a great probability that she would not survive the administration of anesthesia. We were not given high odds for her survival, but we had to try. She deserved the chance. She was eating every hour and had eaten just prior to surgery. The surgeon determined it was not a problem, considering her emaciated state. She was burning up food as fast as she could get it into her system. He was confident enough in his skill that if she did regurgitate food during surgery he could compensate. He wanted her to have the energy to live and food would provide it to her. The reward was greater than the risk.

As Emmi's face was shaved in preparation for jaw surgery, a horrifying discovery was made. The bite that broke her jaw was not the only bite she had sustained. She had dog bites, in various stages of healing, all over her body. The counting stopped at fifty. The worst bite was on her back, between the neck and the withers. It was scabbed and healing but appeared to have bled significantly. Our heads swam with questions. Had these injuries all been caused by her mother? If so, why was she not separated from the mother when the problems started? They were adult dog bites, not that of teething puppies. Why had no one noticed she was injured? Oh, God. What if she had been a bait dog in a dog-fighting ring and had been used to incite frenzied fighting among the larger dogs? We were horrified, angry and wanted answers that we knew we would never get.

When we started her socialization process, the temperatures in Florida were too high to do much outdoors, so walking her in the local pet stores was our best option. One afternoon in Pet Smart, I rounded an aisle with her and came face to face with two brown American Pit Bull Terriers. They were very gentle; they did nothing wrong. They showed no aggression toward Emmi. She, however, was terrified to the point that she cried out like she was being stabbed by a thousand knives and urinated on my feet. It started to give more substantiation to the theory that she could have been a bait dog, but we will never truly know. She had always been friendly to white dogs - Izzy was the best example - black dogs were also not frightening. A blue Weimaraner accidently bit her during puppy class and she shook it off and continued playing. Her good buddy was a grey Weimaraner named Bogie. But if we put her anywhere near a brown or brindle dog of any breed, she shook and urinated. It was unusual to watch this behavior, even as she matured into an adult.

Emmi's surgery took several hours. Her surgical team consisted of a young, intelligent, and very well trained surgeon with two attentive assistants. They took care of Emmi as though she were their own. Her jaw had essentially been crushed on the right side by an extremely powerful bite. The debris from the broken mandible and right arch of her jaw were removed. There was so much debris. And infection. The surgeon cleaned it out as best as he could, but it was weeks old and the bones had already begun to mend and clump together. His estimate was that the jaw had been broken at least two weeks prior to him seeing her. That also gave the infection a lot of time to get established. I cannot comprehend a competent breeder or even a caring back-yard-breeder not seeking veterinary help for such a serious injury. It had to be obvious she was in pain, distress, and couldn't eat. At some point those fifty-plus bite wounds had to have been bleeding. How could it have been ignored? I failed to understand.

Months later, the young daughter of the breeder and her friends messaged me through Emmi's Facebook Page. It was a bit closer to stalking, truth-be-told. She denied Emmi had that many bites. She was adamant Emmi had received wonderful care while in her family's charge. She claimed to love her and wanted her back. I informed her that we had photographs showing the bites and injuries Emmi had sustained. I explained that puppies that were well cared for would not be flea infested and malnourished. The rescue had to get involved. Phone calls were made. It is the first time I ever had to block someone on Facebook. I tried, to the best of my ability, to help this young girl and her friends understand how serious the damage to Emmi had been and what the long-term health consequences were. I felt very sad for the girl and her friends. They apparently had no idea of the full extent of the injuries to this poor puppy. I strongly suggested they volunteer at the local Humane Society shelter and learn about proper animal care. I hoped that they would follow through to gain an understanding of and a compassion for helpless animals.

Emmi was a superstar patient. She never cried once during her recovery. She took her medicine without a complaint. In fact, one of her pain medicines became known in our house as puppy-crack. When she saw us coming with the syringe she almost danced as we shot it into her mouth. Puppies grow quickly and Emmi's healing process was equally rapid. The only issue was the infection, which would not go away. There are very few antibiotics that can be used for puppies. Most have horrible side effects with consequences to their growth. The bacterial infection that was raging in her jaw was not responding to the standard treatment and it was getting worse. Her temperature was elevated and she had puss oozing from her incision.

The surgeon was extremely concerned. He knew something had to be done immediately and there was not a good option available. After several consults with colleagues he decided on a ten-day round of an antibiotic that was known to kill this particular bacteria. There was danger it could cause ulcerations to her cartilage that could lead to permanent damage, but it was the best drug for the job. Ray and I and the folks from the rescue discussed it at length and felt we had no other options. She would die without it. Once again we were advised that the outcome could lead to euthanasia and asked if we wished to continue treatment. We were just a few days into our foster care of this fuzz-ball and our hearts were already captivated. We tried to think logically, but it was difficult. We were in love. Emmi had a way of doing that to everyone she met. She was helpless and damaged, with such a will to live.

Post surgery, Emmi's face looked like she had been on the losing end of a heavyweight-boxing match. Her eye was completely swollen shut. We had to clean her incision every hour to keep the drainage from drying into her fur. She was quiet for the first couple of days after surgery; took her drugs, lapped up liquefied puppy food and slept. At night, Ray and I took turns sleeping on a daybed next to her pen. She was still a puppy, with puppy potty habits, eating a liquid diet.

Liquid in... Liquid out...

Her pen had to stay clean and dry so that her incision remained bacteria free. Fostering her was much more work than either Ray or I had anticipated. It wasn't just a 24/7 job. It was a minute-by-minute contract. We taught her to use a potty pad - a skill she learned quickly and one I was thankful she retained as she matured. It came in handy for stormy weather, which in Florida's rainy season was common. Her aim was impeccable. By the time she was just four months old she was completely housebroken.

During her recovery, we received a daily text or phone call from the surgeon checking on her progress. We all hoped for the best, but prepared for the worst. She had some gigantic hurdles to overcome, but the wounds and incisions finally started to heal. The pus and drainage ceased. After seven days she started to get her puppy spirit back. Once the ten-day round of antibiotics was completed she looked fantastic. The most exciting day was somewhere around day twelve of recovery. Her stitches were removed and we finally allowed Emmi and Izzy to play together. They chased each other around the patio, having great fun playing puppy tag. Emmi ran to one of Izzy's rope toys, PICKED IT UP, and took off at full speed. Izzy was in hot pursuit and they had a short game of tug of war. I didn't get it on video but the images were burned into my brain. It was the very first time she was able to use her jaw since surgery. It had worked! Emmi wasn't very strong and Izzy won the game but she kept at it and looked so happy. Izzy was thrilled to have someone her own size to run and play with. They became fast friends.

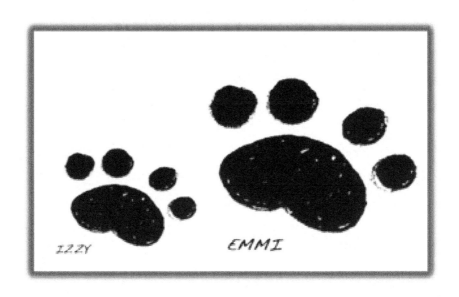

IZZY   EMMI

CHAPTER 6

Izzy's Perspective

Mom and Dad put the fur-ball in the kitchen. Seems kinda dumb to me. It's in the middle of everything. There's no way to get away. I guess I better keep an eye on it. Good thing it's in one of those pen things. Couldn't they keep it outside or something? It's just going to make the house smell like poop. It's probably going to make a mess, too. And steal my toys. I don't share my toys. It can't have my bed either.

Mom and Dad are just sitting here watching it. Mom is on the floor of the pen holding it and trying to get it to eat. Silly puppy. You would never have to force ME to eat. Mom had to put me on a diet once. I ate too much. Everyone said I was fat. Except Dad. He never tells me I am anything but perfect. Mom says he spoils me.

Mom also says I have ADHD, whatever that is. She thinks I am hyperactive. And I lack attention. Not me. I have laser focus, I always pay atten... Wow, there's a SQUIRREL! Oh, what was I saying? Um... Oh, yep. Laser focus. That's me. Have you seen my ball?

Hey, mom is giving it one of my old beds. I guess that's ok. It looks tired. Mom says it needs rest. I think I'll lay down right here next to it and nap, too.

Emmi's Perspective

Boy oh boy oh boy. I like this soft bed. It smells like the Izzy dog. I can curl up here, close my eyes for a while, and feel safe. The Izzy dog is watching over me while I sleep, too. That's really nice to have someone watch out for me. The humans are really quiet. I like it quiet. It helps my head to not hurt so much.

The humans tried to feed me but I couldn't open my mouth so now they are making something that smells wonderful. It's soupy and warm and tastes so good. It's easier to get it into my mouth than the hard food. It's like drinking water, only better. It's making my tummy feel so good. I hope they make me more of this. The man is the one who makes the good food and the lady feeds it to me. I think I like it here. The lady lets me sleep on her lap when I am not eating. She kisses me too. I like kisses. I like to nibble on her nose. It makes her laugh. I like it when she laughs.

The lady says tomorrow I have to have something called surgery. I don't know what that is, but she says it will help my head to feel better. I hope so. My head has hurt for as long as I can remember.

The man and the lady put me in the car again for another drive, to see a different doctor. This one is nice and gives me kisses. He explains to them what he is going to do to me and then he takes me away. I wonder if I will ever get to see the man and lady again? I am pretty used to getting passed around now, so I don't worry. The doctor is very nice to me and gives me a shot that makes me fall asleep.

Ouch, ouch, ouch! That wasn't how I expected to wake up. My face really hurts. And I am getting another shot. The nice blonde girl has something in her hand that smells really, really good. It's food. Yum. And she is giving it to me. Hey! My jaw works. I can open my mouth. I'm eating! She says it is cat food. I have no idea what a cat is, but they sure do have some awesome grub. This is delicious.

The man and the lady are here, too. Everyone is crying. Why is everyone crying? I just want more scrumptious cat food. I have food all over my face but no one is mad at me. They are all so happy. They tell me I look silly and give me so many kisses and hugs. I like all of these people. They don't yell at me or let me get hurt.

The doctor man says I have to stay with him for a while but he will drive me back to the man and lady in two days. I'm not sure what two days means, but I fall fast asleep knowing that I will see them again soon. I dream of my new soft bed and the Izzy dog. We are going to have so much fun together.

There they are! There they are! The man and the lady are here to see me. I'm really excited, wriggling, and wiggling to get to the lady. I like to give her kisses. The man has a beard that is fun to lick. I have lots of stitches and the doctor man tells the lady I have to be quiet for a few days. Yeah, Like that's going to happen. I can open my mouth and I can eat. I want to stay awake all day to eat and eat and eat.

The doctor man is showing them the tooth he removed from a TIGER the day before. It's REALLY big! They all laugh, comparing it to my little tooth that was removed. Someday I'm going to be big like that tiger. Roarrrr.

I give the doctor man a kiss and the man and lady take me away. The lady holds me so tight. I think she likes me. I wonder if I can stay with her for a while. I like that silly white Izzy dog, too. She's fun to play with. But when I get to my bed, it's inside of a fence. I'm not allowed to play with the Izzy dog. The lady says I have to rest. Rest is good. I'm not feeling so well. The Izzy dog lies down beside my bed and naps with me. I think she likes me. I like her too.

My eye hurts! It's swollen shut and it hurts so bad it makes me cry. The lady tells me I have an infection - a really bad one - but the doctor man is going to see me so he can fix it. I like the doctor man. He gives me yummy tasting medicine. It makes me feel better. I am tough and strong.

I. Am. Rottweiler.

CHAPTER 7

My camera was never far from reach as Emmi recovered. I took videos, and still photos constantly. Most were posted to Emmi's Facebook Page. Each day she did something more amazing than the day before. It was as though nothing had ever been wrong with her. She was just a normal puppy. Her weight started to catch up to where it should have been for her age and size. She was beginning to eat kibble, now just softened with beef broth instead of liquefied, and within weeks she was eating un-softened kibble. The surgeon wanted her to use her jaw as much as possible. The hard kibble was good exercise for her jaw muscles and helped to soften the points of her very sharp puppy teeth. We were ecstatic. There did not appear to be any lasting damage from the antibiotics, she was eating well, growing at a nice pace and enjoying life.

It was becoming apparent that Emmi was embedding herself into our life. She and Izzy got along splendidly - a major consideration for making this a permanent situation - and Ray and I knew the medical bills were getting beyond the capacity of the rescue's resources. Fundraising was progressing, but slowly. We were paying many of Emmi's bills ourselves hoping they would be reimbursed but knowing there was a chance they might not.

We suggested to the rescue that we adopt Emmi and make her our responsibility. It was an unusual request so early into a medical foster with unknown bills looming in the future, but we knew we had the resources to continue fundraising for her. What could not be raised, we would pay personally. We decided to make it official and formally adopted Emmi.

Emmi's Perspective

The lady and the man spend a lot of time talking about something called an adoption. They tell me that I never have to live with anyone else, ever again. I am home. I never have to be afraid again and I will get well. They will always take care of me. I have a mom and a dad!! Yippeee!! I think it's pretty cool that they always have food, too. I like food. I am just a little puppy now, but if I eat lots of that yummy stuff, I will grow up to be big and strong just like the missing-tooth tiger.

I will always protect my family.

I. Am. Rottweiler.

When we made the adoption announcement on Emmi's Facebook Page, we were inundated with congratulatory messages and calls. Many were amused that "the poster" was still alive and well. Ray and I have long imagined a poster hanging in Doggy Heaven, featuring our portraits "Most Wanted" style, stating:

If you are sick, injured, or in need
of very expensive medical care,
FIND THESE HUMANS!

One of my dearest friends declared that with Emmi, the poster must now be surrounded by Las Vegas type neon lights, perhaps with it's own laser light show.

Our track record with sick or injured dogs was intact. Our first dog, Kashi, had survived many catastrophes and illnesses in her life, passing from lung cancer at the age of seventeen. Turbo was born with dilated cardiomyopathy - a heart defect. Lexington, Sutton, and Morgan each developed a different cancer. Cooper had the genetic blood-clotting malady Von Willebrand's Deficiency. Gus survived abandonment - living in the woods on his own for almost a year, heartworm treatment, epilepsy, and a thirty-foot fall off of a deck.

With the luck of a cat-with-nine-lives, Madison survived her overactive sense of adventure including but not limited to being hit by a car and thrown fifty feet through the air, getting kidnapped, jumping off a second-story deck onto concrete at six weeks of age, hitching rides on the roof (yes, I said ROOF) of the UPS truck, getting knocked through a plate glass window while playing with Sutton (it almost severed her tail from her butt), getting struck by lightning, opening doorknobs with her mouth and running out into congested downtown traffic, and eating through the power cord of the television (while it was live).

Oh Madison. Life is just not as exciting without you. How you lived to be sixteen years old is a fact we will never fully understand but are grateful for. We miss you every day, sweet baby girl.

And then there was our tiniest "poster" fur-kid... Izzy. We can't forget Izzy. I was quite certain she sat up in Doggy Heaven waiting a long time for us to come along. Few would have tolerated her. She was allergic to the world - requiring multiple medicines and weekly injections of allergy serums to keep her alive. She suffered from early onset cataracts at the age of three, becoming sightless within weeks. Her blindness was caused by poor genetics, created by the irresponsible breeding practices of a puppy mill. But she is ours and we love her despite her illnesses, allergies, specialty doctors, and sometimes-crappy temperament. I'd be cranky too if I had all of her issues.

Yes, indeed. There must be a poster in Doggy Heaven. Would someone please rip it down? And pull the plug on the laser light show, too, while you are at it.

CHAPTER 8

In early 2013, after *Dog-Ma, the Zen Of Slobber* had been published, ending with Izzy's sudden blindness, we discovered that one of her eyes had an operable cataract. It was possible that she could regain vision in that eye if we acted quickly. We had a very short window of opportunity to make the decision for surgery before it started to reabsorb and permanently damage her lens. Within days we had the operation scheduled and began our four-hour round-trip drives to Tampa, FL for weeks of pre surgery and post surgery ophthalmology appointments. Canine cataract follow-up care is much more intensely complicated than it is for people. We had to make an Excel spreadsheet and set alarms just to keep her medicine and eye-drop schedule organized and on time. At one point she was taking eye drops seventeen times a day.

Ray and I were anxious on the day of her post-surgery release. We knew the procedure had gone well, but did not know how much vision she had regained. Would she see blobs and shadows or would her vision be clear? I sat quietly in the room, waiting for Izzy to be brought in to us. Ray paced. Izzy was his baby girl. Our fears vanished the moment Izzy pranced through the open exam room door squealing with delight, recognizing her daddy. She could see!

Just as her world had changed, almost overnight when she was plunged into darkness, it returned to normal at lightning speed. She refused to go to sleep on the drive home. She wanted to soak in every sight she could. Sitting on my lap, she stared out the window, stared at Ray, turned and gazed at my face as if to say "hey I remember you." She was so happy. Our question had always been: did her blindness trigger her nasty temperament with Morgan? Was her aggression based in fear? She started fighting with Morgan after Cooper died. He had been her protector and perhaps she was afraid. Cooper was gone, she couldn't see, and we understood how that could be terrifying. Now that her eyesight had been restored, would she go back to being sweet lovable Izzy? Would the fighting that had become routine in our house continue or cease?

Izzy had to be crated for a few weeks after surgery to keep her quiet and give her stitches time to heal. It was important to keep her blood pressure low. We set up her crate in our dining room - normally a dog-free zone. Izzy and Morgan could see each other but not get close. They seemed OK together. Morgan lay by the doorway, watching Izzy as she slept. It was as though Morgan was guarding her. Protecting her. Being a good big sister.

Yes, that was a fairytale created in my mind. As soon as Izzy was out of confinement the fighting picked up right where it had left off. Nothing had changed. Izzy took every opportunity to pounce on Morgan's head and bite an ear or jowl, only now she had better aim. She could see her target. Morgan reacted the same way she always did and tried to ignore Izzy. She would only bite her as a last resort, in self-defense. Izzy's pink leather muzzle, the "suicide prevention device" was back in full-time use anytime the two of them were together. As long as Izzy wore the muzzle we had peace.

Izzy's Perspective

Wow! I went to sleep in the doctor's office. I think I slept a long time. Doctor Michelle is very nice. She hugs me and kisses me and tells me I am going to be fine. I have funny things covering my eyes like they are taped shut. And I have a silly conehead. I know what coneheads are. I always have to wear one when I fight with Morgan and get stitches. I don't remember fighting with Morgan today. I remember getting very sleepy and... WAIT a minute!

Doctor Michelle is taking the "tapey" things off my eyes. I see light. I. SEE. LIGHT!

I'm so excited. I see all kinds of stuff. It's blurry, but I see the door and the window and the wall and the floor and the doctor AND MY DAD!!! My dad and is here! I am so wiggly I can't contain myself. Dad, Catch me! Dad, dad, dad. I can see you. Dad, dad, dad. I love you.

Oh, hi mom.

We got into the car with lots and lots of medicine. I can't sleep. Doctor Michelle said I would sleep the whole way home, but I can't. I have to look out the window. I've missed seeing so much. There are cars and trees and birds and the beach and the sky and I can't stop looking out the window. What if I go to sleep and I can't see when I wake up? I will never sleep ever again.

Well, maybe just for a little tiny bit.

CHAPTER 9

Over the next two months we began to notice daily changes in Emmi's jaw movement. It was not opening as much as it had after surgery. Eating was taking her longer to accomplish. On a visit to our general vet for puppy shots we mentioned the changes and she felt something in Emmi's jaw that caused her concern. A visit to the surgeon confirmed it. Emmi's jaw was closing. An MRI showed fibrosis and excessive bone growth around the surgical area, possibly a result of the infection she had battled. It infuriated us that a simple round of antibiotics, at the time of her injury, might have prevented all of Emmi's jaw drama.

Another operation to correct the problem was going to be necessary and our surgeon wanted a second opinion from his mentor, a man he greatly respected, who would also assist in a second surgery. We drove two hours to the clinic for an MRI and consultation with The Mentor. After great expense and time, Ray and I both decided this was not going to be the man to lay hands on Emmi. This man told us Emmi would not live to be six months old and would die of starvation. He wanted to euthanize her. We were not going to leave her fate in the hands of someone who did not believe she should be given a chance at life.

Emmi's jaw was closing up rapidly. Within just a few days, meals that had been taking her just three or four minutes to eat were now taking up to forty-five minutes. She had to be fed one kibble at a time, by hand. We tried to go back to the liquid meals but she just made a mess of herself and we worried she was not getting enough nourishment. She could not get her tongue far enough out of her mouth to lap up food easily, with more food ending up on the floor than in her belly. When she tried to use her tongue, it scraped on her emerging pre molars. We knew we had to do something, fast.

Ray and I felt badly, but the experience with The Mentor also severed our relationship with the surgeon. We could not entrust our puppy to a doctor who had any doubt about Emmi's right to survive. We sought the advice of another well-respected veterinary oral surgeon, Dr. Brett Beckman, who primarily worked in Atlanta, Georgia, but once a month brought his team to Southwest Florida. We met with Dr. Beckman and felt an instant connection. He had an aura about him, with animals. A gift. He examined Emmi, read her MRI and CT scan and felt certain he knew what was happening in her jaw.

For a month he tried a method of "staging" her jaw trying to force it open through the use of pressure. His feeling was that fibrosis was forming and if he could break it up with this method he might buy her enough time to delay surgery for a couple of months. If he was successful, it might be possible to get her through the majority of her growth period when the fibrosis would have less chance to re-form. The longer we could delay her next surgery, the better chance she would have at a permanent fix. We took her in three times a week and under sedation, her jaw was pried open more and more each day. She was making amazing progress. Until she wasn't. Her jaw had been opening almost five centimeters and suddenly it was closing down. Rapidly. Something other than fibrosis was affecting her jaw function.

Within a week she could barely open her mouth. Once again we were feeding her small puppy size kibble, one piece at a time. She ate a cup of food - four times a day. Each meal took over an hour to feed to her. It was excruciating to watch her struggle to eat and yet she never showed signs of frustration. She seemed to take her challenges in stride. Always happy. Always sweet. And always hungry. She had grown from an emaciated ten-week old, twelve-pound puppy into a forty-pound tank in a few short months. Our daily challenge was keeping enough calories going into her to support her growth. Emmi's mother had been over one hundred pounds and her father one hundred fifty. She had the genetics to be a very big girl. We often joked that if you watched closely while she slept, you could see her grow.

It was good that she was healthy and growing, but it was also contributing to her jaw difficulties. Everything wanted to grow and it was all growing in the wrong direction and places. Bone fragments that didn't get removed in the original surgery were growing instead of reabsorbing. Torn muscle and tissue from damage and surgery was turning into fibrosis. Her jaw was becoming a clumpy mass of junk. Her growth plates were confused, trying to get her lower jaw to catch up in size to her upper jaw. What was happening to her was not normal or usual. It was as though the bone growth in her jaw was in hyper-drive.

The rapid decline of Emmi's jaw mobility caused Dr. Beckman to contact some of the finest minds in veterinary medicine to gather opinions. He had his suspicions as to the cause. It was rare, unexpected, and something he felt would be best handled in a large veterinary hospital with a surgical ICU team. We appreciated the honesty. We knew he had the talent and capability to do the necessary surgery yet kindly referred us to another facility that had experience with this particular operation. It turned out to be such a good decision. During Emmi's pre-op testing, a deformity was discovered that could have caused her to bleed out within minutes. Guardian Angels continued their watch over our girl.

Dr. Beckman's referral was to Dr. Alexander Reiter at The University Of Pennsylvania's Matthew Ryan School Of Veterinary Medicine in Philadelphia, Pennsylvania. Dr. Beckman and Dr. Reiter consulted extensively prior to our arrival and we felt so well prepared for what was to come.

Philadelphia is approximately a 1500-mile trip from our home in Southwest Florida. Emmi was far too large to fly in the cabin of a commercial airliner and I will never again fly an animal in cargo. Been there, done that. Learned our lesson. United Airlines almost left Madison on the tarmac of Dulles International Airport outside of Washington, DC. In a snowstorm. If Ray had not insisted the pilot open the door and let him check we would have taken off without her. Though I did picture Madison, stranded in DC, escaping the crate (her Houdini skills were legendary) taking herself on a tour of the National Monuments, begging for food from the finest restaurants, and having quite an adventure. She would have loved a rescue by the Secret Service allowing her to spend a few days in the Lincoln Bedroom; dining out of the White House kitchen. Yep, That is exactly how I pictured it.

Realistically, driving Emmi to Philadelphia was our only option. We packed up everything we felt necessary for four days of driving and a weeklong hotel stay. We did fairly well except for underestimating our tolerance for cold weather. Since our relocation to Florida, sixty degree Fahrenheit temperatures felt like the Arctic. We had to stop and buy Izzy a sweater and socks and coats for ourselves. Emmi was quite content with the cool weather. I imagine she would be quite happy in Alaska. Or Antarctica. Or Neptune.

Our drive to Philadelphia was uneventful. The weather was gorgeous and driving through the Carolinas in the spring is wonderful. The flowers planted along the roadside were spectacular. I passed the time on my iPhone. Emmi had been entered in a photo contest where the prize would be donated to the rescue organization that saved her life. I am not a fan of social media contests. I do not feel they are run fairly, in general, but this one had good prizes, even for the lower placing positions so we entered one of her cutest puppy photos.

Much to our surprise, she shot to the top of the contest rather quickly and remained in one of the top three positions throughout the very long four-month contest period. The competition was coming to a close on the day Emmi went into surgery, so I took the opportunity to remind fans to vote as much as I could during our car ride north. It was so much fun. One of Emmi's fans, Dee, made it her personal mission for Emmi to win and sent out messages almost every hour of every day reminding people to vote. During the last few days, she and I got so excited. Emmi was in the lead, by quite a bit, but we didn't want to become complacent. There was another extremely cute dog hot on our heels - another Rottweiler puppy that was also donating the prize money to their rescue group.

Dee and I messaged, texted, and posted on Emmi's Facebook Page constantly during the car-ride north. Several of Emmi's fans got in on the excitement and started to message with us, too. They posted to their network of personal friends and those friends shared. It was so much fun and made our long drive to Pennsylvania pass quickly. We watched the vote count and secretly shared the numbers. We didn't want to tip off the opposition that we were watching. Oh, so clandestine! And their team was probably doing exactly the same thing. We watched every dog in the contest and followed the leaderboard vigilantly. We knew the name of every dog and their vote count for every hour in the last few days.

During the final minutes of the contest the other dog pulled ahead of us and we lost the contest by a bit over one-hundred votes but we felt it had been a fair fight. We gave it our best and congratulated them on a great contest. Several days later the company sponsoring the contest published the official tally. A dog none of us had ever heard of or seen in the contest was announced as the grand prizewinner. The $1000 prize didn't go to either our rescue group or to the rescue group of the other Rottweiler puppy. It went to a dog we never heard of until that moment. It solidified my hatred of Facebook contests.

A former schoolmate secured a beautiful hotel room for our stay - a two-story townhouse just a few minutes outside of Philadelphia. It was a wonderful home away from home for such a stressful week. Emmi had never seen stairs before. Our house in Florida is all on one level, with just one or two steps up. Emmi viewed the steep staircase as a big toy and bounded up with no effort at all. I wish my camera had been ready for her first experience with descent. Suffice it to say, grace was not yet her forte. Paws in front, belly to the carpet, and slide... We could not stop laughing. Izzy, of course, had to run up the stairs and walk gracefully back down as if to say "You derp. Watch and learn. Watch and learn."

Surgery check-in was 7:00 AM Monday morning. We arrived at 6:30 AM, nervously anxious. The waiting room was empty except for the night guard who helped us get settled and made sure we were attended to as soon as the reception staff arrived. He was a sweet man who probably had to deal with panicked and frightened pet parents every day. It takes a special personality to do that job with the empathy he demonstrated.

The clinic was huge, yet homey. Animal portraits decorated the walls along with plaques of remembrance. Reminders that not all who enter leave tear-free. The waiting room chairs were arranged to allow for both privacy as well as conversation. We selected a more private corner, having both Emmi and Izzy in tow. Both girls were extremely well behaved as more furry patients and their humans arrived. Izzy was protective of Emmi, yet on her best behavior sitting on Ray's lap and surveying the room. Emmi was pensive, having been in enough clinics to know what her future probably held that morning. Ray and I tried casual conversation, but we were too nervous to really listen to each other. I struck up a conversation with a woman across the aisle from us whose dog was receiving cancer treatment. We traded canine cancer war-stories. It helped to pass the time. She sent me a note through Emmi's Facebook Page a few months later to tell me her dog had done very well with chemo and radiation and was thriving. I was so happy for her! It is wonderful when cancer has a happy ending.

Eventually, a veterinary student guided us to a consultation room, gathered Emmi's history, and organized all of the records we carried with us from Florida. With great efficiency, she got us ready to meet Dr. Reiter and his Fellowship student, Dr. Maria Soltero-Rivera, who would be assisting him in the surgery. I am not sure what it was we expected when meeting Dr. Reiter. When Ray and I spoke to him on the phone prior to our trip, his thick Austrian accent gave us the mental image of a strict disciplinarian, very business-like and matter of fact, perhaps not the best bedside manner. In person, we found a light-hearted and warm man who explained the upcoming procedure in a way that was simple to understand. He gave us confidence and made us completely comfortable that Emmi was in the best possible hands. He was only technical in his terminology after explaining it clearly in layman's language. I asked a question about the structure in her jaw and how he was reshaping it. Out came a white board and markers. He drew her head from two different angles and clearly explained the probable things he would do during surgery, what complications may arise and how he would handle them. I was envious of his students. They had one hell of a teacher.

Dr. Reiter was not happy with the clarity of the MRI that had been done in Florida and wanted to do his own, as well as an arterial mapping procedure. This would add to the cost of the surgery, he explained, but would give him a much better picture of what he was going to see once he opened her up. Information gained ahead of the procedure would help reduce the amount of time Emmi spent under anesthesia. It would make the surgery safer. Because her jaw was completely shut, they would need to perform a tracheostomy to intubate her for the anesthesia administration and to help her breathe throughout the surgery.

The Plan for Monday:

- Sedate
- Tracheostomy
- Intubate
- Anesthesia
- MRI
- Arterial Mapping
- Surgery to remove the large bony mass
- Wake her up
- Spend the night in ICU

What actually happened was everything up to the Arterial Mapping and surgery was canceled for the day.

We had been escorted upstairs to the doctor's lounge area where we awaited news from Dr. Reiter. It was a great distraction to listen to the veterinary students discuss the lectures they were attending and their work-group discussions afterwards. Listening to some of the health issues they were treating made us realize Emmi's issue, while unique, was just one of many life-threatening illnesses and injuries they dealt with every day. It was humbling.

We were grateful for a quiet place to read and for Izzy to sleep. On the walls were the student photos from each graduating class. I searched for the photo of a childhood friend and quickly found it. I had spoken to him the prior week and he assured me we would be in good hands at University Of Pennsylvania. Students stopped by our seats on their way to class and petted Izzy. They asked why we were there, what doctor was doing Emmi's surgery and always responded with "Dr. Reiter? He's amazing" or "He's the best! You are lucky to have him as your surgeon."

Mid afternoon, Dr. Reiter found us in the lounge. Still wearing his surgical scrubs, he looked concerned and explained that he had canceled surgery for the day. Emmi had been under anesthesia for hours and the complex surgery she needed would take longer than he had expected; not something that could be completed in one day. It would not be safe for her to be anesthetized that long. He explained that there was an artery that was not in the location it was supposed to be and the danger it presented. He showed us the arterial mapping and the empty hole in the bone where the jaw artery should have been located. He explained how, without the mapping, Emmi could have easily bled out during surgery. Arteries are like rubber bands. If one was cut accidentally it might snap back, leaving it un-retrievable, lost inside the mass growing in her jaw. That mass was larger and denser than expected, could not be removed, and complicating the surgery even more was that the mass was attached to her ear structure and skull.

Simply, his original surgical plan would not work. He needed a Plan B and he had to come up with it overnight. Emmi would stay in ICU and surgery would start at 7:00 AM the following day. What had originally had been estimated to be a $3500 - $4000 surgery had now been bumped up to $7500 - $8500. We deflated. Completely. We were so discouraged. We wanted to visit with her but were advised not to. She had an open incision from the tracheostomy and the ICU doctors did not want it to get contaminated. Dr. Reiter assured us he would visit her throughout the afternoon and evening.

For the remainder of the day we struggled to keep our minds off of Emmi. Were we doing the right thing? Were we placing her in more danger than if we had just left things alone? Were we making her suffer? We knew in our hearts that she would die without the operation. Were we being blinded by our love for her and being selfish in our attempt to save her? The comments from our original surgeon rattled in our heads. "You may spend tens of thousands of dollars on Emmi and still have to euthanize her." It was a pragmatic observation. We didn't want her to survive all of this only to need a feeding tube for the rest of her life. Her quality of life would be severely diminished. We trusted Dr. Reiter and felt his compassion for Emmi's situation. We sensed he would advise us if he thought her case were hopeless. We had to relinquish control of the outcome to the surgeon, his skill, and his judgment.

Emmi's surgery had become more extensive and we knew we would be staying in Philadelphia at least a week. It was time to stock up on food. Ray loves to cook so there was no sense in eating out. The best restaurant in town was always Ray's kitchen. We returned to our townhouse after stopping at the spectacular food shop, Wegmans. Ray and I spent most of our adult lives on the West Coast of the United

States and were quite spoiled by amazing grocery stores and local farm markets. In Southwest Florida we were starved for great food stores. Our finest stores were average, at best. I was quite certain when we walked through the doors of Wegmans we heard a full choir of angels singing.

We spent two hours in Wegmans, most of the time either drooling or picking our jaws up off the floor but we were stocked up for a week's worth of meals in our home away from home. Whoever rented that townhouse after us had a very well stocked spice cupboard.

Cooking gave Ray something else to focus on, as well. For him it is his time to relax and de-stress and we both needed some of that. He could bury himself in the kitchen every night and get his mind off of Emmi's condition and the burgeoning cost.

Neither of us slept well that night and we were up and ready to head to the hospital very early. We arrived with plenty of time to find a coffee shop, buy coffee for the parking attendant and the night guard, and wait for the doctors to arrive. We really were not surprised when we entered the doctor's floor and were greeted by both Dr. Reiter and Dr. Soltera-Rivera. We had a feeling they might also be In early. Surgery started shortly thereafter and we thought we would hear some news by noon. At 2:00 PM we started to worry. I was methodically pacing the floor at 4:00 PM when Dr. Reiter came bouncing through the door with a huge smile on his face. Surgery had taken much longer than he had expected and was much more complicated once he got her opened up. He was animated like a child who had discovered a fabulous, yet unexpected, Christmas toy. Dr. Soltera-Rivera was still with Emmi, finishing up. But, surgery was successful. His smile said it all.

SUCCESSFUL! We were so relieved. They had to remove a large portion of her jaw in order to allow it to open and for the left side to function independently from the frozen right side. However, they were able to get an opening of seven centimeters - the most she ever had. Now she would be able to eat on her own, play with her toys, and generally be an active normal puppy. She deserved it. She deserved a normal life. We didn't know at the time how short-lived our joy would be.

Emmi stayed in the ICU until Friday morning. We were able to help feed her and spend time in a private room holding her, to provide parental love. The ICU nurses were very attached to her and when we were in the private room would stick their heads in at least every two or three minutes to check on her. It was endearing. They told us that on Emmi's first night after her lengthy procedure, Dr. Reiter crawled into her cage and talked to her for a while. He held her gently in his arms and told her she was going to be OK. Emmi had a way of bringing that out in people. She was special; such a big lug, yet so fragile.

Throughout our first two days of surgical challenges, I tried to keep her Facebook fans informed and posted hourly updates. I tried to be upbeat and positive. The amount of supportive comments and private messages I received back was heart-warming. So many fans that lived near-by wanted to stop in and meet us. The college from which I graduated a zillion years ago wanted to do a story about our experience with Emmi for their newsletter. They had a veterinary program that worked hand in hand with University of Pennsylvania's program and they thought it would be exciting to do a photo shoot with Emmi and some of their students. I felt guilty saying no. No one realized just how stressful this was on us. We tried to keep our public face bright and cheerful through social media but we were actually terrified. Emmi was our only concern. We were not good company and we looked like crap.

One fan was persistent. He worked only blocks from the hospital and messaged me frequently that he would like to meet up. Even if it was brief. He was a childhood friend of the folks who run the rescue that saved Emmi so we said yes, of course. We finally connected on the last day we were in Philadelphia, just as we were checking out with Emmi. John was able to come back to the exam room with us, meet Emmi and spend a bit of time with us and with her. He made a very generous donation to her massive hospital bill, which was unexpected but greatly appreciated. We felt like we made a friend for life. It was heartwarming to see someone as emotional about her as we were and to experience, even for a few short minutes, the trauma she had been through.

Our drive back to Florida was long. We didn't get an early start and hit horrible traffic as we passed through Baltimore and Washington DC. Our initial plan was to drive straight through to Florida, in order to make it easier on Emmi. We didn't want to move her in and out of the car unnecessarily. She was drugged, dopey, and we just wanted her to sleep. What should have been an achievable sixteen hour drive, between two drivers, became obvious after Washington DC that we would have to stop for the night and find a hotel. The rainstorm we were caught in slowed traffic to a halt. We had not packed the car with the intention of stopping, so the only things accessible were dog food and dog accouterments. We found a hotel close to the highway, slept in our clothes, and just flopped for the night. I was worried about infection with Emmi and asked for extra sheets so we could make a clean spot on the floor for her. The night manager was so accommodating when I explained why. We all got a good night's sleep and a safe early morning start.

Though we were not able to make the stops we initially planned in order to visit friends, we got home in one piece. One episode with a backseat full of pee was our only drama and relatively speaking that's not bad. Somewhere in Orlando, FL a restaurant cleanup crew opened up their dumpster and found a really wet, stinky dog bed. Sorry. Emmi was not comfortable going to the bathroom on a leash and definitely not in the rain, while drugged. She held it for as long as she could. I'm sure it was at least a gallon of pee. Thank goodness at the beginning of our trip we had lined the seat under her bed with potty pads and towels and had a spare dog bed in the back of the car.

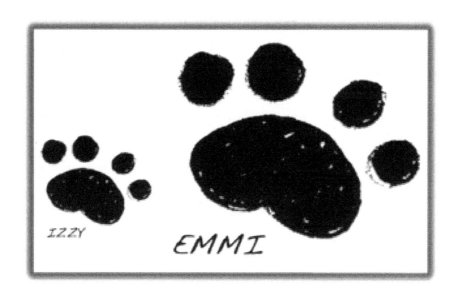

IZZY

EMMI

CHAPTER 10

Izzy's Perspective

Philadelphia is cold. I don't like to be cold. I haven't been this cold since we left that San Francisco place. It was cold too. And foggy. But we had a neat yard. On a hill. I could chase birds and squirrels and stuff. One time I jumped off the second story deck to catch a bird. Mid flight. I got it! And I got stuck under a big bush, chasing a critter. Dad had to use hedge clippers to cut me out. I wasn't scared though. I'm brave. I'm not a scaredy-cat like Cooper was when he saw a BIG deer at our front door. Uh oh, I'm getting off topic again... ADHD is so challenging...

I like my sweater. I'm glad that mom and dad bought it for me. Mom picked it out. It's warm. I would have been an ice cube without my sweater - a ridiculous terrier ice cube. Not cool. Not cool, at all. Now I want boots. And a scarf. And a hat - one of those cool beret hats. I think I would look awesome in a beret hat. Mais oui! Oh wait. I'm not French. I guess I would need Wellingtons and a Flatcap. Not as cool...

At home I wear sweatshirts in the winter. One of them has a skull and crossbones on it. Like a pirate! Aarrr! Dad bought for me. He knows my style. I have some really pretty sweaters from when mom and I used to fly in airplanes a lot. I don't like my pretty sweaters. What does she think I am...a girly-girl? Sheesh... Silly mom.

The dog hospital is fun. Lots of people pay attention to me. I am worried about Emmi but don't tell mom and dad. I need to keep up appearances of being a tough girl. There are lots of doctors and nurses here who give me hugs. It's nice not being the patient for a change.

We are staying in a really nice place in Philadelphia. I've stayed in hotels lots of times. I'm a traveling gal. Mom and I stayed in hotels when mom worked and I went everywhere with her. But we never stayed in a hotel like this. This is like a house. It has a fireplace that makes me warm and a kitchen so dad can make us dinner. And it has stairs. A big set of stairs. Emmi tried to walk down them, and fell. Splat.

She's so silly. No coordination. I showed her how it's done. Gracefully. Head held high. One paw in front of the other. I could take two stairs at a time if I wanted to. Three, or maybe four! I'll have to teach her some athletic skills when she is better from her operation. I miss her. She's the coolest little sister in the world. I hope she gets better soon so we can play again.

WAIT... Maybe she's not cool after all. On our way back home to Florida, Emmi PEED.

In. The. Car.

Disgusting. How uncivilized. Mom says she's sick and to cut her a break. Nope. Ick. I'm so embarrassed by her. Eeewwww. I want a new sister!

Emmi's Perspective

The doctor man in Philadelphia is called Alex. I like him very much. He is kind and gentle. He tells me he will fix me and I should not be afraid. He sits in my cage with me and hugs me and talks to me. I am not afraid. Really, I am not. I miss my mom and dad, though. I haven't seen them for two sleeps. There are lots of nice nurse people taking care of me, but I hurt. I have a tube in my throat so I can breathe and I don't like it. I pull it out and the nurse puts it back in. Alex tells me I have to stop doing that. He lies in my cage with me to make me feel better. I like his voice. It helps me go to sleep.

The nurses put me on a giant-sized wheelie bed and I get to go for a ride to a big white room. It has really bright lights. I'm not afraid, but I sure do wish mom and dad were here. The white room is so cold and bright. I'm not afraid. Really, I'm not. Alex is there and he tells me to go to sleep and when I wake up I will see my mom and dad. I'm not afraid. I'm going to close my eyes now. I want to be brave.

Mom and dad are here! Alex told the truth. I woke up and here they are. I am so happy. The nurse tells me I can't get so excited and have to stop wiggling but I don't listen. Not until I give mom kisses and dad a hug. We get to sit in a special room, made just for me. Mom gets to feed me and it is so much fun covering her with food. Heeheehee. I just got food in her curly red hair.

I have a funny blue cone on my head and a tube coming out of my leg where they put in medicine to help me get better. The tube in my throat is gone, but there is a hole. Mom's kinda grossed out by the hole. The doctor tells her it will heal up better if they leave it unstitched and he teaches her how to clean it until it is healed. I am so happy to see mom and dad, but I'm tired and need to go back to sleep. Mom tells me we are going home tomorrow. I miss home. I'm going to close my eyes again and dream.

It's going home day! It's going home day! My jaw is working. I can eat! I'm so excited to see mom and dad. The nurse takes me to a room where mom and dad are waiting with the doctor. I get to meet Mr. John. He's very nice. I gave him lots of sloppy kisses. Mom whispered in my ear that Mr. John helped pay for my surgery. That was nice. I will give him more kisses. We get all kinds of instructions for our car ride home; get stocked with food and medicine. Dad made me a super soft bed in the back of the car for the trip and he is so gentle as he lifts me up into it. We are going home. Yay!

I'm very sleepy and just want to close my eyes. I dream I am brave. I dream I am strong. I dream...

I. Am. Rottweiler.

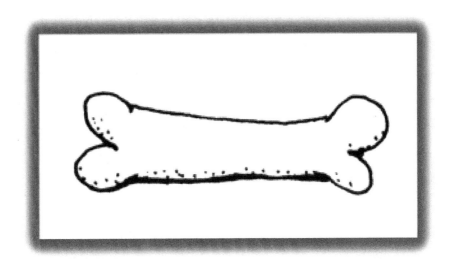

CHAPTER 11

E mmi healed very quickly. Within days she was running around, picking up toys, playing with Izzy as though nothing had happened. She was joyous when she was able to pick up and run with her favorite stuffed monkey for the first time in months.

Physically, the changes were more obvious. Some teeth had been removed, her tongue hung sideways from her mouth instead of out the front. It didn't matter to us. She was beautiful. The dip in her jaw where her tongue hung out would keep her alive. It eventually became the only way for her to get food. Whether Dr. Reiter developed this as his Plan C for "what if all else fails," we do not know, but it kept her from needing a feeding tube as her jaw problems progressed.

Over the next two months we watched with heartbreak as Emmi's jaw slowly closed. It was gradual but we could see weekly changes that concerned us. Her baby teeth had not yet fallen out, as her adult teeth began to erupt through the gum line. As they got larger, they began to puncture her soft palate, something both Dr. Reiter and Dr. Beckman had warned us to watch for. There was a smell - just an awful rotting smell that first alerted us to the problem. Her largest and most developed canine tooth was the first to puncture and fester. It was impossible to clean properly, even though we brushed her teeth daily. Reaching this part of her mouth was just not achievable and we knew it must be painful. The time for surgery number three had arrived.

Dr. Beckman felt an aggressive extraction would be the best long term solution and planned a removal of all canine and incisor teeth. This would leave her with only the teeth from the mid part of her jaw and back - the premolars and molars. No teeth would remain that could puncture her soft palate and cause another infection as she matured. We scheduled the procedure for a date two weeks in the future and during those two weeks watched as her jaw completely froze shut. It was alarmingly rapid.

Dr. Reiter mentioned in the recap of his surgery that while reading her MRI he observed an unusual skull thickness. He said it could be nothing and she could grow out of it but it should be something to watch. This observation was prophetic. What had happened and caused the rapid repeated closure of her jaw was a condition called calvarial hyperostosis accompanied by cranio-mandibular osteopathy. Both conditions manifest as excessive accumulation of the bone surrounding the brain, the ear, and the lower jaw. They were most likely triggered by the infection from the original bite she sustained. The one that she received when her jaw was crushed. The bite from her canine mother. The bitch. Literally. It would never be known conclusively but was theorized that if that original infection had been treated immediately with proper veterinary care, the challenges she faced would not have occurred. It made me want to scream. The irresponsibility of the breeder was beyond my comprehension. It was a complete disregard for another's life.

The new jaw closure that Emmi faced was not on the right side. The broken side. The side where she had undergone two operations to give her comfort and mobility. Now the problem was on the good side. Her left side. The undamaged, never-operated-upon side that should never have become a problem. It was solidifying into a mass of bone. Frozen shut. We watched her go from total function, playing, eating and being a normal puppy to not being able to open her mouth even an eighth of an inch. The lockdown had become so severe that when Dr. Beckman did her pre-operative examination he determined the tooth extractions had to be done through the gum-line. It was not possible to extract the teeth in the normal manner. A simple straightforward surgery had now become not only urgent but also more complex.

Dr. Beckman consulted with Dr. Reiter as well as other colleagues around the country and putting their collective brilliant minds together came up with a plan for Emmi's future. Dr. Beckman performed Emmi's third surgery in July 2014 - a second mandibulectomy to disconnect the left and right sections of her jaw and the tooth extractions. The bone that Dr. Reiter had removed in Emmi's second surgery had grown back. Every effort had been made and precaution taken to prevent this, but she was a growing puppy and puppy bone wants nothing more than to grow. As Dr. Beckman explained to us, if you put two pieces of puppy bone in a room, in opposite corners, they will find a way to grow together. Build a wall and the bones will grow through it. That is exactly what happened to Emmi. The bone grew back. To exacerbate it, the overgrowth of bone, the hyperostosis, had taken over the good side of her jaw preventing it from working properly.

Had this same injury befallen an adult dog, none of these problems would have occurred. The crushed jaw would have healed and with antibiotics the infection would have never taken hold. If a mandibulectomy had to be performed, one operation would have sufficed. The bone would have been wrapped in cartilage, the area would have healed, and the bone would not have grown back. In a puppy as young as Emmi, her body wanted to grow. All of her growth hormones were firing. Broken fragments of bone thought they were supposed to grow, and they did. Into one big clump of junk.

As we proceeded through the first six months with Emmi we began to grasp why so many of the doctors had advised euthanasia. We finally understood the unbelievable odds she faced. Our original surgeon had consulted with professors at his Alma Mater. They had only seen one case like Emmi's and the puppy did not survive. The doctors at Penn Vet had only performed this surgery on eight puppies of her age. Ever.

There was a 60% chance she would not survive the surgery and an even lower chance that the surgery would work long-term. Dr. Beckman felt that because she had survived to six months of age, we had a fighting chance. He knew we were dedicated. And just a little nuts. We were not people who backed down from a challenge. If anything, Emmi's impediment drove us forward, seeking answers and a positive outcome.

Ray and I struggled with the decision for a third surgery. Not because of the expense or even because of the pain Emmi would endure for a few weeks. Our concern was whether or not we were doing the right thing for Emmi's quality of life. The decision was not simple. We knew the teeth puncturing her soft palate had to be removed. That was a given. They were festering and would impact her overall health in the immediate future. And they had to hurt like hell, though Emmi never let on that she was experiencing discomfort. We both realized that she had known nothing BUT pain for most of her life and she probably thought it was normal. What we struggled with was whether or not it was fair to her to keep subjecting her to medical procedures. Were we doing it for her, or for us at this juncture? It was a dilemma. We lost a good deal of sleep in the week leading up to the third operation.

Dr. Beckman was realistic in his evaluation. He made us aware of the odds, the possible complications, and what her future life would be like if the surgical result was one of worst-case scenario.

Surgery day arrived. Emmi's prep began before dawn. The overall procedure went well, though there was a mid-surgery change of strategy. Dr. Beckman conveyed the unfortunate news that Emmi had indeed developed hyperostosis. It prevented him from separating the two sides of her jaw leaving her with less movement and function than planned. He hoped for a small improvement but warned us her jaw would never function properly. With hyperostosis in control of Emmi's jaw and skull, there was nothing he could do to help her gain more function. It was as though her entire jaw had become encased in concrete. Dr. Beckman was successful in removing all of the impinging teeth so she would no longer have a risk of infection from a tooth puncture. He hoped the front teeth extractions might encourage her tongue to work more normally and have space to move in and out of the front of her mouth as needed rather than continually hang out the side.

Emmi spent one night in the ICU and we brought her home the following afternoon. She was dopey and not as spirited as we had expected. She wasn't peppy like she was after surgery at Penn Vet. This operation had been harder on her and, in all fairness, she was coming home much sooner. In hindsight we should have let her remain in the ICU a day or two more.

Her first day and night home were uneventful. She slept. She ate a little. She whined from the pain medicine - something we had become accustomed to with Rottweilers. They can get very "talkative" when recovering from anesthesia or with certain medications, so we were not overly concerned. There was no need for her to be uncomfortable after surgery with so many wonderful pain medicines available. Dr. Beckman is an advocate for proper pain management, having published several papers on the subject. Emmi was prescribed oral as well as injectable opiates to keep her comfortable.

The second day following her release from the hospital we saw a frightening backslide. Her whining escalated to crying. She could not settle down and sleep. I laid down on the floor with her and attempted to keep her comfortable. She refused to eat or drink and she had not urinated in more than thirty-six hours. I was terrified as her health rapidly declined. When the light and sparkle dimmed in her eyes we realized she had stopped fighting. She was exhausted and was giving up.

Ray and I knew if we did not do something immediately we were going to lose her. At 4:00 AM. Emmi had a temperature of 105 degrees. I took a short video of her behavior and texted it to Dr. Beckman. At 4:30 AM he called back and requested we rush her immediately to the clinic. He called ahead to alert them to our emergency allowing the on-call doctor to be prepared to treat her immediately. Emmi had developed an allergy to the morphine she was taking for the surgical pain and compounding her distress, pneumonia had taken hold. This poor girl did not need one more thing to battle. She spent the next four days in the ICU clinic with round the clock care.

Emmi's Facebook Page became quiescent. I could not post anything about her condition without bursting into tears. I always wanted to keep the page upbeat and positive and there was nothing good about this situation. My inbox was bursting with messages asking for health updates. With the page this silent, her followers knew something was wrong. During Emmi's Penn Vet surgery her Facebook Page was buzzing with updates; photos of Izzy in the waiting room in her cute button-back sweater, what we had for lunch, the conversations we overheard from the students - silly things to keep her followers apprised that everything was fine.

When her page became totally silent, her fans realized something bad had happened. They posted comments expressing their concern and suspected things were dismal. I texted a few close friends to inform them of the situation. My intuition was playing games with my logic. Emmi was getting the best care possible, I had confidence in the doctors, but my gut told me we were losing her. Our fear was that our good fortune with Emmi's resiliency had run out.

Ray and I made many two-hour-long round trips to the clinic to sit with her, hold her, and encourage her to fight. Her eyes were blank. She recognized us but seemed detached. Her little nub of a tail would wag periodically, just once or twice before she ran out of energy, as if to tell us she was doing her best. We knew we were in the way but we didn't particularly care. We were not going to allow her to die without us present. She had been through so much and deserved to have us with her. The ICU nurses told us they talked to her constantly hoping it would encourage her to fight. One stayed by her cage, continually monitoring her vital signs. Every visit broke our hearts just a bit more. She was so ill and not improving.

Connie asked for permission to post an update on Emmi's Facebook Page in my absence. She posted the facts. Emmi was in dire condition in the ICU and the unanticipated costs were skyrocketing. Once again our Facebook family came together. Connie organized a Yard Sale prior to the second surgery to help offset costs and did an amazing job raising over $2000 toward the Penn Vet bill. Misfit The Blind Dog held an auction for Emmi raising $1200 toward the third surgery. Emmi's You Caring fundraising site was humming with activity, which was helping to cover our planned medical bills, but four additional days in the ICU caught us off guard. Through the generosity of Emmi's virtual family, within twenty-four hours we received enough donations to cover her entire ICU bill. We were grateful to have one less thing to stress about that week and so thankful for the friends we made through our social network. We were both emotionally and physically exhausted. Having the burgeoning medical costs taken off our responsibility-plate was appreciated beyond words.

Emmi was weaned off the morphine and placed on a drug that her system could better process. It did not offer as much pain control, but helped to keep her as comfortable as possible under the circumstances. The antibiotics began to fight the pneumonia and after two days her fever finally broke. Once again, Emmi had a guardian angel watching over her, though this time I think they took up full-time residency and brought a few extra angel friends for assistance.

She was weak but she was going to live. Emmi had lost an alarming amount of weight. The ICU technicians were challenged at feeding time and got used to being covered head to toe in Emmi muck. She got more food on them than into her mouth but with their persistence, she ate enough to regain some strength. She came home weak and thin, but alive.

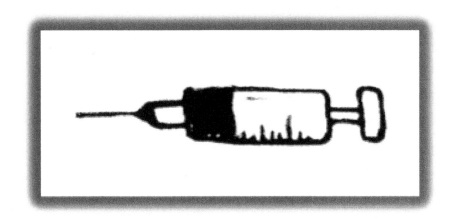

CHAPTER 12

Emmi's Perspective

I don't feel very good. When I woke up from a big sleep, my mouth hurt so much. I have a conehead again. Pleaseeeee, take it off. I promise I won't scratch my face. My head already hurts and this cone thingy is making it worse. Where's my mom? She would understand and make the nurse take it off. I'm a good girl. I know how to behave after surgery. I'm a little pro but too sleepy to think about it right now. I think I will close my eyes, just for a minute. Just for a tiny minute.

Mom and dad are here! I am so excited to see them. Mom says that I hurt now so that I can eat by myself. I hope, I hope, I hope. That would be amazing. And it would be great if I could play with my toys again, too. I want to go home. I miss my monkey friend.

Wait! They are leaving after kissing me goodnight...

NO mom! Don't go! I promise I will be good. Take me with you...

The nice nurse wakes me up and keeps trying to feed me and she doesn't understand why I won't eat. My tummy feels terrible. I think my medicine is making me sick, but I can't make anyone understand. I want my mom.

Maybe if I go to sleep mom and dad will be here when I wake up...

"Emmi, wake up."

I hear mom's voice. It hurts so much to open my eyes, but I try. Just a little bit so I can see her. I give her the best kisses I can manage, but it hurts... even to kiss. I am so happy to see dad and mom. But I really don't feel well. I heard mom say I am going home today. I better put on my brave face so I don't have to stay here one more minute. I want my own bed and my own bowl and my own yard and my mom. I want my mom.

It's so good to sleep in my own bed again. I am trying hard to be Rottweiler-Strong. I really am. But I keep feeling worse and worse. I close my eyes to sleep but I am so sick I can't sleep. Mom is lying on the floor with me tonight and I like feeling her hand on my foot. She makes me feel safe.

I'm so hot. I need to tell her but I'm too tired. Maybe if I lick her nose she will understand. Oh, yay. She is getting me some ice. I like ice. It makes my tummy feel good. She knows. Mom understands.

Oh, this ice doesn't make me feel good. Ew, ew, ew. I threw up. That burns my throat. I am fighting hard, mom. I'm sorry to make you so sad. I'm fighting, but I'm tired. I don't know if I can keep fighting much longer.

I'm trying not to cry mom, but I can't help it. Mom, please don't cry too.

The cool cloth on my tummy feels good. Dad puts me on the cooling gel-pad that my Auntie Helen sent to me. That feels nice. I hear mom and dad talking to the doctor man. I am pretending to be fine, but mom knows I am sick. Really sick. I am coughing and can't catch my breath. Dad lifts me up very gently and puts me in the car. He's being as tender as he can, but even his strong arms makes the rest of me hurt too. It's ok dad. I know you want to help.

I am tough mom. I don't need the doctor. I just want to go to sleep. Please just let me go to sleep. I don't ever want to wake up.

Mom tells dad she is terrified. I've never seen mom this sad. Don't worry mom. Please don't be sad. But right now I want to sleep. I need to sleep...

It seems like days have passed. Every time I wake up I look around to see if I'm home but I'm still in the hospital. I see mom and dad for little bits but then I go back to sleep. I try to tell her "I am strong mom! I can fight." But then I'm not sure if I can. I hear a voice while I am sleeping that tells me to fight, to concentrate really hard to get better. The voice tells me I am loved.

The nurses are all very nice to me. They let me sleep, except when they feed me. They use a big shooter thing to get food gently into my mouth. It's not fun. I get food all over my face. The nurses try to help but I am messy and they laugh at me. I like it when they laugh - it makes me happy. They say food will help me to get better, but I'm not very hungry. They said I could go home if I eat so I am trying really hard. I want to go home. I miss my mom.

I sleep again. The voices return, telling me that I'm going to have to fight harder to get better. They tell me I am loved by so many and I was put on this earth for a reason. To find out the reason, I have to get well. The voices give me comfort.

I dream of running and playing with my toys. I dream of eating my dinner all by myself. I dream of mom smiling at me. I dream I get stronger. I fight as hard as I can to get better so I can take care of my family. That's why I am here - to teach them courage, to protect them with my whole heart.

I. Am. Rottweiler

CHAPTER 13

Emmi was very thin and our first order of business once she came home from the hospital was to get some weight back on her. Without any front teeth her only food options now were liquid. The ICU technicians had suggested using a large syringe to feed her, which I tried and failed with, miserably. It was messy and I was concerned about shooting too much into her mouth and having her aspirate. I did not want her to have another bout with pneumonia caused by liquid getting into her lungs. But most importantly Emmi needed independence. Rottweilers are very gallant animals and Ray and I felt by hand-feeding her she would lose some of her pride. We watched that happen when she initially had trouble eating her kibble and we had to hand her one piece at a time. She was frustrated that she could not do it herself and would struggle for five minutes just to get one tiny piece into her mouth. We didn't want to see that happen again. We had to teach her how to drink her food neatly, get it into her mouth, and not all over her face... and the walls... and the floor... and the ceiling... It took some time and patience.

Some of her eating success depended on us creating the correct food texture and that could only be accomplished by trial and error. By letting her eat small batches at a time and giving her large amounts of praise for going slow, savoring each lick and getting the food into her mouth, she gained confidence. Once in a while, especially if we missed an exact mealtime and she was particularly hungry, she gulped and made a mess. This was why she ate either outside, if the weather permitted, or in the middle of our spacious walk-in shower. There's a lot to be said for a room you could just hose down. And for a dog that LOVED a warm shower.

Emmi developed a method to drink water from the handheld shower nozzle. It cleaned out her mouth after meals as well as provided hydration. It took a lot of effort from her to get a drink from a bowl of water. Her tongue did not curl under to lap water like a healthy dog's. Emmi's tongue simply pulled in and out. Her dipstick method worked for food, but water was too thin to stick. Her preferred method of drinking was to use the hose or the shower wand. She figured out the right angle for the water to get in and not choke her. She truly was a clever girl.

We finessed her food blend as she grew and as she approached adulthood it changed again, concentrating on nutrient dense foods and supplements. Since all of her food was put into a food processor and blended, we added fresh fruit and vegetables, meats, and nutritional oils along with her adult kibble. We chose grain-free Orijen Six Fish kibble and softened it with salt free homemade beef or chicken bone broth. She received a heaping tablespoon of organic coconut oil daily along with cranberry powder, since developing a UTI from her daily swimming sessions. If we didn't have fresh fruits or veggies appropriate for her we added organic stage-1 baby food vegetables. We wanted her diet to provide balanced nutrition with a variety that would stave off boredom. Could you imagine having to drink a liquid diet for the rest of your life? It would be awful. We wanted her to enjoy her eating experience while having the nutrition she needed to grow and stay strong. She loved Carrot Monday and would dance in the street for Kale and Beet Thursday. With each meal she got a few tablespoons of a pure protein, either buffalo, duck, turkey, beef, venison, or rabbit. One discovery we made is that Emmi hated salmon meat. She wouldn't touch it. She had no problem with other fish varieties, which was amusing since salmon was the main ingredient in her kibble. She was quirky.

The same Lisa that sent Emmi her Snuggle Puppy®, suggested adding Golden Paste into Emmi's food as she approached adulthood. It is a powerful antioxidant, a natural anti-inflammatory, protects from cancer and helps to keep a dogs system running efficiently. We make our own from organic ingredients and add it into Emmi's meals every day.

Brushing Emmi's teeth was a daily necessity that, of course, all dogs should be subjected to. None of our dogs ever enjoyed it, but it did help to keep their gums and mouths healthy. I think it was a contributing factor to the longevity of Kashi, Gus, and Madison. Each of them surpassed fifteen years old, which, for large breed dogs is unusual. For Emmi, it was critical to make it a part of her daily routine. Gingivitis could have led to a host of other infections and since she could not move saliva around her mouth easily would be more prone to it. Traditional doggie toothpaste was too thick for her to swallow easily. We tried several brands and all had the same results. Once she choked, she wanted nothing more to do with the toothbrush. After many experiments, we settled on dipping a toothbrush directly into coconut oil. It is a natural antibacterial and is very effective in fighting gum disease. Best of all, she loved the flavor and no longer tried to have a wrestling match with the toothbrush.

Cooper

CHAPTER 14

Emmi had great instincts from the day we brought her home. She seemed to understand immediately that Izzy was one to be honored and respected. Her friendship was something to be earned. Emmi learned quickly that if you were nice to Izzy, Izzy would reciprocate. Most of the time. Well, sometimes. Truth be told, Izzy would be nice if all of her personal planets were in alignment. If they were not, all bets were off. Emmi seemed to instinctively know Ray was a pushover. If you licked his ear he would give you the world. Her Rottweiler instincts for protection would develop as she grew. Our other Rottweilers developed their natural guarding and herding behaviors between the ages of one to two years, so what happened on Emmi's first day inside our fenced yard was extraordinary.

We had a neighbor we did not care for. We believed he was involved in the actions that led to the death of our Doberman, Cooper. Unfortunately, our fenced dog yard is adjacent to his yard. Following Cooper's "accident" Izzy had refused to use the dog-door or yard. She was with Cooper when he was injured. Izzy was small and could use a potty pad. It was never a big deal for us to accommodate her and quite frankly we didn't want her in the yard taking the chance she too could have an "accident." Emmi would become a very large dog and needed to learn to use the yard for her bathroom duties. We wanted her housebroken as early as possible and began yard familiarization immediately. We would never leave her outside unattended but wanted her to know that this was the proper bathroom place. She was just over twelve weeks old and very undersized for her age when I introduced her to the grass. I carried her down the three steps knowing she was much too tiny to navigate them on her own, and placed her in the grass. She sniffed and looked quite content. I was sure there were still remnants of those who have grazed those grasses before her - Madison, Morgan and Cooper. She took a deep breath and filled her lungs with everything there was to smell, familiarizing herself with her new surroundings.

Then she froze. The hair on her hackles stood up and her nose lifted to sniff the air. She growled. Her chest reverberated from a rumbling in her throat that bellowed out like a sonic boom. It was ferocious. Over and over. She charged the fence and would not stop

94

barking. This tiny puppy was defending her home. The bad neighbor was standing on his patio watching us. I ran to her, picked her up, and whispered in her ear "good instincts sweetie." She licked my face in acknowledgement. Her young eyes conveyed her adoration, grateful feelings for being saved, and her desire to be the family protector.

As she grew older, wiser and significantly larger she did not bark at the bad neighbor. She only alerted us that he was outside, then simply stared at him; always placing her body between us when we were in the yard. She did not like this man and instinctively knew he had caused our family pain. Emmi was our sentry. She was friendly with everyone else she met. A little too friendly, oftentimes. We were working on that.

Izzy's Perspective

I had to warn Emmi about the man that hurt Cooper. I was there. I saw what happened to my bestest buddy in the universe. I could never tell mom and dad with words. We terriers don't have verbal words. I told them with my heart. I showed them that I was afraid to go in the yard by myself. I always kept a laser-focused terrier-eye on that guy when he was outside. I'm not much good at protecting mom and dad. I'm too little. But now that I have a new sister, SHE will take care of us if I train her right. She's gonna be BIG.

Emmi's Perspective

Mom thinks I have good instincts, but it was Izzy who told me about the bad man. She warned me and told me what happened to the Cooper dog. How the bad man hurt him and he never came home. As soon as I smelled that man I knew I had to defend mom and dad. I let him know not to mess with me. I may be little now, but just wait Mr. Bad Man. I'm going to get really big someday. I take my family protection responsibilities very seriously.

I. Am. Rottweiler.

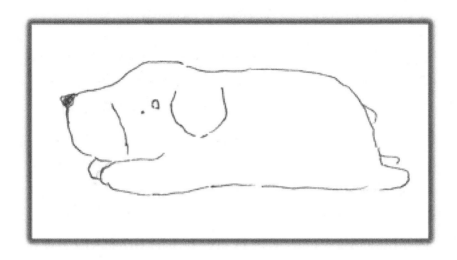

CHAPTER 15

Every sixty days, or so, Emmi seemed to have another medical crisis or emergency. It was a bit of a curiosity for our general veterinarian, Dr. Sandy. Her job was to keep the rest of Emmi's body healthy while the specialists fixed her jaw. Emmi kept Dr. Sandy VERY busy. Those who followed Emmi's Facebook Page also noticed the pattern. It was curious.

In September 2014, two months after her third jaw surgery, Emmi found herself at Dr. Sandy's again with a sudden and unexplained limp. It appeared to fluctuate sides - one time on her left front foot and later that day on her right front foot. She had a distinctive bob of her head when she walked, indicating something hurt. She had not fallen or been injured, she had nothing stuck in either of her feet; she was not cut and had no signs of an insect bite. We kept her toenails filed very short and eliminated long nails as a cause almost immediately.

The X-ray she ordered was troubling to Dr. Sandy, causing her to consult a neurologist who confirmed her suspicion. Emmi had spinal damage, consistent with what you would find from "shaken baby syndrome." We could only assume it was from her canine mother violently and repeatedly shaking her as a puppy; perhaps at the same time her jaw was broken. Then we remembered the photos that were taken before her first surgery and recalled one of a bite between her shoulder blades. It was the worst of all of the bites on her body. The photo showed a scab covering almost two square inches on her tiny little body. It resembled a burn more than a bite, but many bite wounds surrounded it. Was it possible that this was the bite that damaged her spine?

Because we had Emmi in a training class and had been using a training collar instead of her harness for corrections, we had irritated this old injury. We had caused our baby pain. We didn't know. We would never have knowingly caused her any pain or discomfort but still felt horribly guilty. I was so angry and took the training collar and threw it in the trash. There was a great debate between factions of dog trainers. Some believed that training collars, used properly, were not painful. Positive reinforcement trainers believed training collars were pernicious. We fell somewhere in between. For a large breed dog who is physically out of control and stronger than the owner it could be a good tool if used properly. On a smaller dog it was grievous.

Ray and I shared our home with many dogs through the years. Big dogs. Each had been trained a bit differently but all had behavior that was exemplary. Well... Except for Madison - our Houdini-in-a-dog-suit. There wasn't a thing about her behavior that could be considered exemplary. Madison's behavior was nothing short of breathtakingly ornery. She was spirited. We never used a training collar with her, but in hindsight it may have saved her from herself. We were asked to not return her to puppy class after only two days. How bad does a dog have to be to get kicked out of PUPPY CLASS? That's like failing pre-school. One experienced trainer we later hired declared her un-teachable and that she must be of low intellect. We could actually see her laughing as she pranced all the way to the car after being kicked out of Board and Train for barking non-stop. She had barked so much that it caused severe laryngitis, which left her with a permanently raspy bark. So proud, she was.

Suffice it to say, except for Madison, we never needed to utilize a training collar in our thirty-plus years of dog guardianship. Yet, with Emmi we felt like idiots, as though we had never trained a dog in our lives. Then we realized why we felt so challenged... Her name was Izzy.

The Germans, as we had collectively called all of our Rotties and Dobies, had trained their younger siblings when they arrived in our home. Kashi was our original dog of German lineage. She was professionally trained at The Academy Of Canine Behavior in Washington State along with Turbo. They were both perfectly mannered. Kashi trained her new buddy, Lexington, after Turbo passed away. Madison, Gus, and Sutton were trained by Lexington. Sutton trained Cooper. Cooper trained Morgan. The domino effect is mind boggling, isn't it? Yes, of course we did the training or had help from some well-respected professionals, but each dog had a wonderful "example-dog" to follow. One that responded to a command the first time, every time. Training was always easy and I think the strong foundation that Kashi learned and passed down through generations of dogs made it easy for us to have a full house of large dogs with nary a behavioral issue. Except for Madison, of course.

Madison's response to commands were as follows:

Leave It - Put it immediately in mouth and chew. Swallow the evidence.

Come Here - Turn and run as fast as possible in the opposite direction from which the command originated.

Don't Leave The Yard - Run next door and play with the chickens, all the while barking a sing-song version of "neener, neener, neener, you can't catch me."

Quiet - Become the center of attention in any way possible, including yodeling.

Sit and Stay - Dance around like a clown until the command generator hangs their head in disgust and walks away.

Then there was Izzy - the apple of Ray's eye - a seventeen-pound wild, crazy terrier terrorist. Cooper was her protector, but he never taught her a darn thing about German philosophy. Morgan wasn't sharing either. Izzy was spoiled, coddled and sick most of her first two years of life. She was a hellion. And she was now Emmi's behavioral example. As Emmi's trainer said, "God help us all."

When we first allowed Izzy and Emmi to play together, we exercised extreme caution, not wanting Emmi to sustain any further injuries. Izzy's history with Rottweilers was a concern. Emmi had been through some sort of dog bite situation and we didn't want to exacerbate any residual stress. They stayed separated most of the time with Emmi in an exercise, or Xpen, and Izzy free to see, touch, and smell. The times they were together they were highly supervised. Some of the earliest video I have of the two of them is adorable. Izzy was initially unsure, Emmi was a typical puppy, and both ended up running and playing like best friends. Emmi convinced Izzy that she was an awesome toy!

We consulted with an animal behaviorist immediately and had her come to our home for an afternoon. We wanted her to observe both dogs to see if there were any behaviors we were not picking up on and should correct. She felt that Izzy showed the appropriate leadership skills and correction techniques when Emmi played too roughly, shared her toys well, and would be a good role model. Emmi showed respect for Izzy's authority and ownership of all things on the floor. Her final analysis was that they were absolutely fine together and would become great friends. I later wondered if she had been smoking crack - my personal favorite phrase for "was she nuts?" As she grew and matured, Emmi and Izzy were as far from best buddies as two dogs could get. Not because they didn't like each other, but their size difference didn't allow for safe play.

One of the many virtual friends I had on Facebook was Mary Blanton from 2 Dog Trail Positive Dog Training in Colorado. Mary provided me with so much free dog training advice over the years I probably owed her an all expenses paid trip to Florida - but she would come visit and get wrangled into more training. When I posted about Emmi's injury, if it is possible to yell virtually, Mary yelled at me. Positive training is all about reward based training, not training collars. She was so disappointed that we had chosen the training collar route, yet I explained that Emmi was like a cross between a freight train and a hippo. We had spoiled her while she was a manageable size and now we had a seventy pound spoiled brat. It was our fault for not disciplining her when she was small, but she had surgery after surgery and it always seemed that just as she was healing and ready for classes something else happened that put training on the back burner.

We couldn't use treats for training - my excuse to Mary - because all of Emmi's food had to be liquid. I made excuses about there not being a liquid high-value treat. I rationalized that training collar. My excuses were epic. I also really personally liked the trainer we were using. She was very good with Emmi and she had gained Emmi's respect.

Mary yelled. Loud and clear. And I thanked her for it later. Mary quickly sent me a link to a product called a GoToob and suggested I order one, fill it with pureed tripe and use it as Emmi's high value treat.

Yep, it worked. Yep, it was messy. Yep, it was stinky. Most importantly, Emmi loved it. It helped training get back on track.

Emmi was far from perfect but was making progress, especially with houseguests and people who regularly worked around our home. Without the use of her jaw she felt that she couldn't defend herself or her family. As a Rottweiler this must have been her ultimate frustration. Her solution became jumping on people to demonstrate her strength with what we referred to as her World Wrestling Federation moves. She still had her dewclaws. Her bear hugs hurt. We slowly broke her of this habit by rewarding her when she kept all four feet on the floor. No one was permitted to scratch her butt or rub her ears until she calmed down. We were teaching her to trust.

CHAPTER 16

Izzy and Emmi's relationship was wonderful when they were of a similar size, but as Emmi grew it became more tenuous. And Emmi grew quickly. She gained a pound every two or three days after her first surgery and she was growing like a weed. Gangly, yet well proportioned. It never occurred to us that her jaw would close up again and we were not concerned with her being underweight. The pounds would catch up to her eventually, eating a well-balanced diet.

Original Morgan had always been overweight. She was confined to little activity for her first two years of life with shoulder and CCL surgeries every six months. At one hundred and sixty five pounds, she was simply fat. We had allowed it. It took almost a year of the green bean diet and lots of walks to get her down to a proper weight, though it was never easy for her. She battled weight issues her entire life. She was certain she was being starved and abused when Cooper got a bowl of kibble containing three or four heaping cups and hers had one measly scoop. She was always hungry. Some of it was from being so overweight as a youngster and some of it was probably genetics, as it is with humans. Either way, we didn't want that to happen to Emmi.

We watched her weight and food intake militantly, keeping her a bit on the lean side. Sadly that became a huge issue as her jaw began its second closure in March 2014. When it was time for her Penn Vet surgery, she was significantly underweight. Even with the effort we were making, hand-feeding her four hours a day, she was not getting enough calories to grow. A mistake from which we learned. As we prepared for her third surgery we beefed her up with additional calories and I am sure it is the only reason she had the strength to survive the negative reaction to the morphine and pneumonia.

Because of her immobile jaw, Emmi was unable to pant and cool down like most dogs. She overheated quickly making long walks unsafe. In South Florida our summer Fahrenheit temperatures were in the upper nineties and in the winter averaged in the seventies. Emmi tolerated walking for about five minutes before she started to overheat. We tried cooling scarves and spray bottles containing cool water. Connie even made her a beautiful cooling jacket. But they did not cool her down sufficiently to keep her safe.

One of Emmi's biggest fans is Helen. We met through Emmi's Facebook Page and found out later she lived not far from where I grew up in Pennsylvania. When she heard about Emmi's difficulties cooling down she had an idea. She read about a cooling gel-pad from The Green Pet Shop that was self-recharging and stayed cool for hours. She thought it would be helpful for Emmi in the summertime as well as for emergencies; especially if we lost electricity and therefore air conditioning. She bought one and had it shipped to us. That cooling pad got tremendous use in the summer of 2014; power failures, high fevers from infection. It was a godsend.

An advantage for Emmi, living in South Florida, was that we had a swimming pool. Dogs cool themselves through panting and through the pads of their feet. With this in mind, Ray designed our pool for the dogs we had at the time. Big dogs that loved water. It had large steps on each end of the lap-style pool for easy access and egress. They were wide enough for a large dog to relax on and take a nap in the summer heat. Our first dog, Kashi, learned the value of a nap in the water while living in our Los Angeles home and we wanted to recreate that space for our current and future dogs.

When Emmi was a baby, we needed to teach her not only how to swim, but also how to get out if she ever fell in accidentally. Izzy had the same lessons, hated the water, and would not swim willingly. But she was taught exactly how to get to the closest steps to climb out on her own if an accidental swan dive occurred. Periodic drills would bring on the stink eye, pointed in my direction, for days afterward. These drills became lifesaving when Izzy's eyesight suddenly failed.

Though she was a great sightless navigator, Izzy would occasionally miss the edge of the pool and fall in. She knew if she swam in a straight line she would find a wall and if she followed the wall she could find a stair and get out on her own. Even with her Safety Turtle alarm blasting it's alert throughout our home, we were sometimes far from the pool when it went off. Izzy generally found her way to a stair before we arrived to pull her to safety. She was never afraid of the water but did not like to get wet. Conversely, Emmi took to the water like a fish. We never had to put a life jacket on her to let her learn how to paddle. She loved it from the moment she first got wet. An audition at Sea World, as The Canine Mermaid, may be in her future.

I initially set very strict rules for the pool and Emmi, seeing how much she enjoyed it. "Go swim" was the command letting her know it was ok to get in. She was only allowed to enter the pool walking in from the steps, no jumping in, or diving, and was never permitted to enter from the side. Additionally she was never allowed IN the pool unless a person was in the pool first. We started with a half hour a day, learning proper pool etiquette such as don't dunk the human and no, it's not ok to try to ride on the human's back. Emmi became a strong swimmer very quickly. We have a seat along the middle edge of the pool called a "swim-out," something required at the time our pool was built as a place someone could use as a safety area in the deep end. It is ridiculous since drowning people could never hoist themselves up onto it from deep water, but it does serve as a wonderful deep-water seat for Emmi. She rapidly learned "steps" and "middle" as commands for where she was to go. "Swim to me" took some time, but she eventually mastered it.

Emmi could not pick up toys from the water. Even during the times her jaw did somewhat function, it never opened enough to grab a toy in the water. A cheap $2 green Styrofoam noodle became her favorite pool buddy. She pushed it from one end of the pool to the other like a tugboat operator, docked it in the swim-out area, and then continued on to the steps. It was a playtime routine we had for quite awhile. She also enjoyed having it thrown halfway down the pool to chase, but only if I would race her to get it. She loved the competition, loved winning, and on occasion when I beat her to the noodle, learned she had to be a stronger paddler. We swam laps together for a while, but she found them boring and turned laps into a game of "I am now going to jump on your head and pull your pony tail so I can beat you to the steps." Our girl is quite the competitor. And cheater. Our neighbors laughed when they first heard me call her "Cheater-Pants." They thought I was talking to Ray. It didn't take long for them to become accustomed to hearing me chat to Emmi all day long.

The first pool video I posted of Emmi prompted one new follower to respond with a suggestion to help her become a stronger swimmer. He had noted that Emmi did not use her back legs to kick and only paddled with her front feet. He was a certified canine hydro-therapist and thought it was perhaps because she had an injury and could not use her back legs. He was concerned for her safety while swimming and was trying to offer genuine guidance. He mentioned that dogs use their back legs to keep them afloat much like people use their arms to tread water. It is necessary for them to stay horizontal and not have their butts drop, pulling them underwater.

It was curious, and I had not noticed it previously. It became my obsession for weeks. I would touch her back legs while she swam and do a push-pull with them along with the command "use your legs" to give her the idea for how to use them. Her response was usually an annoyed glance. She used her back legs as a rudder to navigate and make turns but rarely used them to move through the water.

Teaching her to use her hind legs was apparently unnecessary. She knew HOW to use them. The issue was that when she did, she always beat me to the toy we were playing with. She was throttling her speed so I could keep up. When I challenged her to a real race with the "use your legs" command she won. Every time. She cut through the water like a hot knife through butter.

While cleaning out our garage, Ray stumbled upon a toy - a small blue rubber ball tied on a neoprene slingshot, called a Go-Frrr. I think we received it as a gift for Izzy, thought she would just destroy it, and put it away in the drawer full of miscellaneous dog stuff. Ray thought it might be a good pool toy for Emmi if it would float. She might be able to maneuver her snout inside the neoprene loop to retrieve it in the water.

Well, it took her all of thirty seconds to figure it out. I floated it in front of her, stuck my hand through the loop, and pulled the ball out of the water hanging the loop over her nose. The excitement in her eyes was mind-blowing. She knew exactly what to do with the ball. I placed it in the water a few feet in front of her and she lowered her head, pushing her snout into the loop. It took her a couple of tries, but she got it. I threw it further away and she swam for it. This time she captured it on the first try and swam back to me with a look of accomplishment and pride I will never forget. Emmi could now play her first game of fetch-the-ball. The blue ball became invaluable in teaching Emmi commands such as "retrieve," "leave-it," and "mine." It became an integral part of our daily swim/play/train time.

The blue ball also gave Ray a brilliant idea. Using his giant Mensa brain, he figured out how to attach tubing to other toys so that she would have more variety of playthings she could actually carry and not just push around with her nose and feet. He made toys she could play with in the water or on land, which allowed her to carry them with her snout. Emmi was lucky to have such a smart and thoughtful dad.

Emmi's love of the water and Izzy's polar opposite hatred usually allowed Emmi playtime on the pool deck sans Izzy, who would find a nice quiet (and dry) spot in the house to relax while Emmi swam. One afternoon Ray and I were working in the yard, keeping an eye on the girls from afar. All was quiet as they both relaxed in the shade inside of our pool enclosure. Our next-door neighbor had just adopted a shelter puppy - an adorable, but bark-happy, ten month old Spaniel mix boy named Toby.

Toby was being walked around his back yard, on leash. He was new to the neighborhood and had not yet met his doggy-neighbors. When he saw Izzy and Emmi he naturally started barking, which threw Izzy into one of her infamous chaotic tantrums. Emmi jumped up to see what all the commotion was about, accidentally bumped her now seventy pound hulk of a body into Izzy's tiny seventeen pound delicate frame and Izzy went flying into the pool. And I mean, FLYING. She emitted a high-pitched, ear-piercing shriek as she vanished into the deepest waters. Emmi thought it looked like great entertainment and followed after her. Izzy's banshee cry must have been heard for miles. I had never seen Ray run that fast. Ever. By the time we reached the edge of the pool, Emmi was using Izzy as a bobbing toy. Up and down... Up and down. Though she knew how to swim and escape the pool, Izzy's head was not above the water often enough for her to catch her breath and she was panic stricken. Emmi had no idea why so many people were screaming at her to stop pushing Izzy underwater. She was just a girl having fun.

I've lost several iPhones due to their lack of submarine capabilities. My first was lost diving into the pool, fully clothed, with an iPhone in my pocket to rescue a drowning Madison. We believe she had a stroke before she fell in, sinking to the bottom without a struggle. She made no attempt to save herself. Her rescue and resuscitation were thankfully a success. The rice immersion for my phone was not. The second dip in the pool for an iPhone was simply leaning over to get one of Emmi's toys and - PLOP. The phone fell out of my pocket and gently fluttered to the bottom. I confess. I was a serial killer.

As I was running at full speed alongside Ray, I did manage to throw my iPhone into the grass and kick off my flip-flops, which made running just a tad easier. It was truly quite an accomplishment for the world's biggest klutz and I received high praise from Ray for not breaking a bone. Trying to swim and use lifesaving techniques on a panicked mouthful of gnashing teeth was challenging. Ray grabbed Emmi from the pool's edge and held her in place so I had a chance to get Izzy to shallower water where I could stand up and assess her welfare. She was frightened but fine. A few hugs from her daddy would fix everything.

Sadly, that was the last day Izzy and Emmi spent any significant time together. We realized that as much as they enjoyed each other's company, their size difference was too dangerous. Emmi was a typical klutzy puppy and Izzy, still blind in one eye, was overly protective of her personal well-being. We would have to keep them separated for their safety, at least until Emmi was no longer a puppy. Emmi was relegated to the south side of the house, yard, and pool-deck and Izzy had the north side and kitchen. At night, Izzy slept with us and Emmi had the run of the rest of the house with a bed under my desk in the kitchen. Not ideal, but we made it work.

CHAPTER 17

Raising a puppy is not for the faint of heart. It is a lot of work, even when a puppy is totally healthy. Feeding, training, housebreaking, cleaning up the mess when housebreaking fails the first nineteen-thousand times, multiple daily walks, vet visits for puppy vaccinations, de-worming, and the inevitable "my puppy ate" visits to the vet. (Insert your own experience here. Our list included car keys, phones, socks, chocolate bars, bubble gum, an entire Thanksgiving turkey, full bottles of medications, and appliance power cords). It is an enormous responsibility to protect them until their common sense kicks in. The challenges multiply exponentially when they are as sick and damaged as Emmi.

Thankfully, the one thing we never had to worry about was chewing or eating something she shouldn't. We had many other worries far exceed that one, but a non-chewing, non-thieving puppy was quite a novelty for us. Over our many years of puppy parenting we have lost the corners of walls, entire cabinets, chair legs, stair treads, an irreplaceable vintage table, seven sofas (five to one dog – our beloved Kashi), and more socks and underwear than I can keep track of. Dobermans got the moniker Doberthieves for a very justifiable reason... Someone "borrowed" my entire Victoria's Secret spring collection and buried it in the front yard of our Tennessee home. Cooper stole and buried a phone in Oregon that never was found. What a time capsule "find" it will be someday for a little kid making mud pies in the backyard. Lexington ate straight through a wall in our Seattle home into the side of a bathroom cabinet, for no particular reason. The look on his face when we arrived home said "But mom, it was THERE! I just couldn't help myself." Burp...

We would have gladly accepted all the damage in the world, in trade for Emmi's functioning jaw, but on the bright side, her affliction saved us many typical puppy repair bills. The downside was that we had to be her 24/7 entertainment committee. She couldn't be told to go lay on her bed and chew her bone. We couldn't fill a Kong toy with frozen goodness and let her guttle it for a couple of hours to keep her busy. We were it. We were her muses. We kept her from dying of boredom.

Emmi was, thankfully, quite intelligent. She learned quickly and had fun conquering new tasks. She invented new games on a weekly basis.

During the hot summer months, all games centered on the pool. She would often get aggravated when she was trying to teach me a new game. How's that for role reversal? Emmi-soccer became a daily ritual of powerfully and accurately placed shots. Her blocking skills at the goal were admirable. While swimming one afternoon, she adapted her soccer skills into a new pool game. We had been playing a round of chase-the-ball-to-the-opposite-end-of-the-pool, when she decided to jump out of the water to retrieve a different ball from her toy bucket. She kicked it into the water like a well-trained athlete. I thought she wanted to change balls so I threw it to the other end of the pool for her, promptly getting harrumphed. Back she went to the toy corral for another ball, kicking it into the pool. It took a few more attempts for her to conquer my stupidity until it occurred to me what she wanted. The entire pool was the new goal and I was the goalie. Ding, ding, ding. From the water I was supposed to roll the ball onto the patio for her to block and then she would try to get it back into the pool. My responsibility was to block the ball from the water. She got very clever, taking the ball to the far end so that I had to swim hard to block it. When I got tired, she was kinder and kept the ball closer to me or in the shallow end. She loved it when I would shout out the score and high-five her for a well-won goal. Our neighbors thought I was nuts. Simply bonkers. Once in a while, life got in the way of Emmi's designated playtime only to leave us managing through her energy bursts at night. We learned early on that a tired dog is a happy dog. And one that would sleep peacefully through the night.

Izzy was very fond of her extensive collection of tiny orange and blue basketball style Chuck-It Balls and she was rarely seen without one in her mouth. Emmi played with them when Izzy was not watching and chased them around the kitchen using the island and cabinets like a skillful pinball wizard. She could entertain herself for hours with a Chuck-It ball. One afternoon on the patio, Izzy dropped a Chuck-It ball, leaving it as a tempting treat for Emmi. With very few obstacles to bounce it off of, Emmi got frustrated as it landed repeatedly in the pool. It did not take her long to figure out how to stop it by grasping it between her paws and placing her head on top of it. A new game was born. The Goalie Catch transferred to her other toys and allowed her much more independent play. She expanded her skills with the finesse of Mia Hamm.

CHAPTER 18

Facebook Pages is such a large community of people coming together with common interests. We've received amazing support, comfort, and advice on Emmi's page. The majority of her devotees felt like our extended family. We laughed together on great days and cried together when things did not go according to plan. Every photo or video that was posted on her Facebook Page had likes and comments almost immediately. The majority of those words were kind and supportive. Many of her regular followers frequently responded with "I love her" or "look how happy she is." We knew each other's dog's names and quirks. We celebrated new puppy additions to the family and together mourned the passing of the sick or elderly. We were truly a virtual family united by our love for Emmi.

Every once in a while, things got ugly. It happened on the day I mentioned that Emmi was not feeling up to snuff and had not eaten her dinner. One of her fans, who was a medical doctor and knew Emmi's history extremely well, suggested she might be getting ready to go into heat. A firestorm of criticism erupted from those I called "the ones who stand on their invisible soapbox and bash."

"Why is Emmi not spayed?"

"Do you know how irresponsible that is?"

"Emmi could have an unwanted litter of puppies. How ghastly!"

My inner snark began to rise up. Surprisingly, I was quite aware of how puppies were made and the precautions that needed to be taken if and when Emmi began her heat cycle. One of my friends suggested I just ignore it, delete the posts, and forget about it. Another thought it would be very amusing to announce we had found the perfect mate for Emmi - a handsome Chihuahua - and we were going to start breeding a line of Rottiehuahuas. Another friend with a dry sense of humor and a beautiful Australian Shepherd offered up his services for Rauttsies, though as she said, sadly, his ship had sailed. He was neutered. Some would have seen the hilarity and some would have been horrified. What I did was politely explain the situation.

"UPDATE: To the many asking about her not yet being spayed, it is a

very complicated surgery for Emmi and her jaw surgeries have taken priority. To give her anesthesia she needs a tracheostomy which, by itself, is major surgery. With her allergy to morphine painkillers, it is going to be a horribly uncomfortable recovery for her. She needs a break from all of that right now. She will be spayed. Just not yet. Believe me, there's no one who is looking forward to her heat cycle LESS than me. She is always confined to our home, there are no unneutered male dogs in our neighborhood, and she has no chance of becoming an unwed mother. None. Don't worry."

The apologies began rolling in.

"I didn't understand her condition completely."

"I'm so sorry. Thank you for educating me."

And my absolute favorite response to all of the nonsense:

"Let those standing on their soapbox drown in their own bubbles. You've got this girl."

Our Facebook family was a bit fractured, but educated. Emmi would not get spayed for some time, if ever. That decision would be up to her primary veterinarian, Dr. Sandy, along with us. It would have to be safe for her to undergo anesthesia and her pain would have to be managed properly and humanely. There were several surgeons Dr. Sandy suggested, whom we could interview when the time was right.

There were studies that show many breeds, Rottweilers included,

119

lived healthier and longer lives when not spayed until after several heat cycles. It was thought to prevent bone and muscle maladies, cancers, and many other health problems. Breast cancer continued to be best prevented by spaying, but when done at the age of eighteen to twenty-four months. We had time to make our decision. The veterinarians we spoke to throughout Emmi's various surgical procedures generally agreed that delaying her spay would be advisable. There was not a "life critical" need to do it and allowing all of her hormones to develop fully could help her in the long run. Mostly we just wanted to give her a break and some time to just be a dog, without a health problem. She earned it. She deserved it.

On the day that her heat cycle started I didn't panic. I thought I had a game plan. First and foremost was to get her into a tiled floor room - easily cleanable - until I could access the full breadth of the situation. We had not yet purchased any supplies for her so I started making a list.

√ washable doggie diapers

√ light days feminine pads

√ washable cover for her bed, our bed, and her favorite sofa

It was not a complicated list to fill until we called our local Pet Smart and discovered that doggy diapers in XXL were not an in-stock item. Nor were they at PetCo or our locally owned pet store. Emmi was huge, sporting a twenty-seven inch waist. I should have thought this through a bit in advance. I was generally a compulsive planner but for this situation I wished she would stay a baby just a little bit longer. I became an ostrich with my head in the sand. La, la, la.

Ray and I, in our thirty odd years of dog-raising, had never dealt with a dog in heat. All of our females had been spayed and males neutered. We were in unknown territory. My first call was to Dr. Sandy, who assured me, with great confidence, that we could handle this newest hurdle. Seriously. As a woman, I knew the drill. But this was my little Emmi. My fragile little Emmi was becoming a grown up. The sanitary and safety issues were obvious and something we had thought about in advance. We hadn't considered her tendency towards urinary tract infections or how this would affect her daily swimming routine. Dr. Sandy assured me that we would be fine. Emmi would need her own sanitation department for two or three weeks and swimming would be just fine for her, especially in the salt-water pool as long as she was very dry before her diaper went on. It was November, the weather was perfect for Emmi to be outside most of the day, so she and I hung out, swam, played, did a bit of gardening and kept her diaper free until night-time.

I let Emmi's "inner circle" of Facebook followers know early in the day what was happening and they had some great suggestions; one being little boys underwear, turned backwards using the flap opening for her tail. It was an excellent recommendation, though the style choices in boys XL were limited to pirates and pirates and pirates. Someone reminded me that since we live in South Florida, a female pirate was perfectly acceptable. I was certain that someone would come up with a fantastic pirate name for her by the end of the day. Many fun monikers rolled in but I never could decide on a favorite.

Eventually I posted the big event for her Facebook followers to see, along with a picture of her in her pirate panties. So many helpful suggestions were posted, not only for other options for sanitation but also advice on how to cope. One of her fans had me laughing like a deranged lunatic. We were discussing "flow" and she said her own dog's first heat was very light and she hoped that Emmi's was as well because when her daughter's dog had come into her first heat cycle "You would have thought someone chopped up a cow in the house." It was reassuring to know others shared my warped sense of humor.

Emmi's heat cycle lasted for a bit over three weeks, right through the Thanksgiving holiday when we hosted a houseful of visitors. Her pirate panties were a big hit with our daughter's friends from France. Les Pantalons de Pirates received many laughs. They thought little boy pants for a girl was genius.

Our five-year-old neighbor had so much trouble understanding why we were not going to have puppies, as she desperately wanted one. Her mother, on the other hand, was immensely relieved.

Emmi was not the same carefree puppy when her heat cycle ended. She was nervous and seemed constantly worried. It was a personality change that caused us concern. When she began trying to burrow into the sofa cushions, we recognized the symptoms of nesting. Her hormones told her she was going to have babies. She was creating a place to whelp her litter. Emmi was having a false pregnancy. We knew there was not a chance in the world she was actually pregnant and watched with amazement as her belly swelled and she began producing milk. Dr. Sandy said, while unusual after a first heat cycle, a false pregnancy was not a rare occurrence. We filled Emmi's usually unused crate with soft bedding that she could snuggle into and allowed her to do what an expectant mommy should do. She rarely left her bed and after a week she began pacing, panting and appeared wildly uncomfortable. A quick text to Dr. Sandy confirmed what we suspected. FALSE LABOR. Good grief. Poor girl. All of the pain of a pregnancy and none of the reward. Within a few hours Emmi was exhausted but sleeping. It was all over.

We gave her two rubber squeaky toys to act as her "babies" which was an enormous error in judgment. She bopped them with her nose and pushed them under her bedding. The squeaking made Izzy and us insane. If I tried to take the babies away and put them in a drawer she became visibly agitated. Note to self... if this ever happened again the faux babies would be silent. After a few weeks of twenty-four hour noise, Emmi awoke, pushed the babies out of her bed, and slapped them with her paw so hard they flew across the room. The babies were on their own, banished from her bed. She returned to her normal silly self.

CHAPTER 19

Emmi was maturing into an extremely confident young lady. Florida is the lightning strike capital of the world and even our huge thunderstorms did not wake her. If thunder crashed right over the house, she might lift an eyelid. Maybe. She was such the opposite of Izzy, who was fearful of most everything. Emmi quietly observed something she did not understand before reacting. The things that got her attention in a less than positive manner were TV shows with loud voices or when men were demonstrating violence toward women or children. She once growled angrily at the TV during a particularly savage episode of *Game Of Thrones* when a horse was being harmed. Her issues were not fear based, but protective in nature, as Rottweilers are generally inclined. She may have witnessed violence by men when she was a puppy or retained fear from the event which resulted in her broken jaw. However, I never considered her a fearful dog. She was strong, bold, and self-assured, which is why the event during our Thanksgiving festivities in November 2014 caught us off guard. Up until that week the only fear we observed was of brown pit bull type dogs.

Our South Florida home provided a beautiful setting to celebrate an outdoor Thanksgiving feast. The cool fall temperature allowed us to light a wood fire in the outdoor pizza oven to help stave the chill. As soon as Emmi saw the flames she brimmed with terror. Her eyes bulged. With ears pinned tightly to her head, she bolted to the house - to the safety of her room. Shaking violently, she fearfully sunk into her bed and could not be consoled. I did not understand what had happened and tried to provide comfort as I sat with her on the floor. One of our guests had observed the panic on Emmi's face at the moment she first saw the fire. We tried to coax her back outside to face the fear but she would not leave her room until the fire was completely extinguished.

We were not certain if it was the smell of the burning wood or the sight of the dancing flames that triggered her fear, until several weeks later. Because our indoor fireplace in Florida is rarely used, for years we have filled it with large battery operated candles. Emmi was with us in the kitchen by the time the candles turned on every evening and she had never been exposed to them. Earlier in the day I had changed the candle batteries and had not yet returned them to the living room.

When Emmi saw the multiple "flames" turn on one by one, she fled to the safety of her bed, again shaking uncontrollably. I brought two of the candles to her so that she could see they posed no threat. She urinated. All over me. All over her bed. For some reason, flames were terrifying to her. We did not know why. What she experienced in her first ten weeks of life remained a mystery to us but we suspected there was a very bad trauma involving fire. It broke our hearts that we were unaware and that our actions had reignited such an enormous fear. I had visions in my head of her tied up near a campfire while dog fighting went on all around her. It would take a great deal of time and desensitization before she was able to conquer her pyro-phobia.

Posting issues such as Emmi's fear of flames on her Facebook Page often stirred up anger within the ranks of her ardent followers. So many wanted to know why the breeder was not prosecuted for cruelty to animals. Some posted that they wanted to go meet him to introduce a baseball bat to the back of his head. Violence would not have solved anything. The breeder needed to be educated not punished. When Connie accepted the puppy into rescue she did her best to provide counsel and strongly suggested Emmi's mother be spayed. If her mother could do such a great amount of harm to Emmi, it could be in her genetic makeup and not something that would enhance the Rottweiler breed if she whelped future litters.

A few months after Emmi's adoption, a puppy of similar age appeared in a "for sale" ad on Craig's List. A local friend noticed the ad and saw the resemblance to Emmi. They could have been twins. With a bit of clandestine investigation it was confirmed that it was a puppy from Emmi's litter. She had been returned to the breeder because she was too energetic - a condition Ray and I were all too familiar with. I wished we could have adopted her but so many, including our veterinarian, advised against it. Littermates, especially females, are not good long-term housemates and we already had the Izzy "wildcard" in play. Rottie Nation Rottweiler Rescue tried to no avail to get the dog into their custody so it could be placed into a proper home. I hope she found a happy, loving, and safe home to live in for the rest of her life.

CHAPTER 20

We experienced a vast mix of emotions with Emmi on a daily basis. We felt such empathy when she tried to accomplish a simple task for the average dog, yet for her a monumental struggle. And we had unimaginable joy when she succeeded. She learned to use her front paws like hands with her toes substituting for fingers. Though her meals were prepared into a slurry of liquefied nourishment, for training treats we occasionally used Izzy's kibble. It had a unique texture that when moistened by Emmi's tongue, became easy for her to swallow. We placed one at a time into Emmi's mouth like a coin slipping into a slot machine; her tongue drew it down her gullet. A dropped piece of kibble could have been heartbreaking, yet because we never coddled her and allowed her to accept her challenge, she devised a system to return it to her mouth. It was normal to watch her pick up a piece of kibble between her toes, place it on her tongue, and swallow with accomplished pride.

As she matured, Emmi developed a routine of sorts. Breakfast on the patio followed by a short swim. Naptime lasted until sometime around "I am too bored to stay inside and I demand attention NOW," anywhere from 10:00 AM to noon. That's when I would don my swimsuit and head to the pool with her. Her creativity in inventing new games was astounding. She never played with the same toy two days in a row, except for her orange inflatable beach ball. It was her best friend. She wrestled with it on the sofa, played soccer with it on the patio, and bounced it from her nose like a seal. When one got damaged we had a closet full of spares, thanks to some very generous friends.

Ray watched us one day when we were playing in the pool and was astonished at her accuracy. If a ball got knocked out of the pool, she ran after it and kicked it back into the water, soccer player style. The first time he witnessed it; he thought she got a lucky hit. But after observing us for a few hours he realized Emmi had about a ninety-five percent accuracy rate in returning the ball. Not just in the vicinity of my location, but directly in front of me; often right on top of my head. Her aim and distance judgment were spectacular.

When Emmi had her third operation and she was well enough to play but was still not cleared for swimming, we needed to come up with a playtime activity for her to burn off some energy. She had her fill of indoor training and games of hide and seek. She wanted to be outside. To keep her brain and her body tired, we bought her a giant rubbery Yoga ball. It was larger than she was tall and if under-filled with air, the ball became soft and squishy. She had to figure out how to make it play with her which solved the brain exhaustion dilemma. She pounced on it and rolled it all around the yard. Pushing it with her nose, she could bounce it high when she made a well-placed hit. It became a favored yard toy. She loved splaying her body on top of it and then slowly rolling to the ground like melting chocolate. It provided awesome fun for her until she got too hot and would have to go inside to cool down. We had to watch her closely for heat exhaustion when she played outdoors. She never knew how much activity was too much. It was a very fine line.

Finn

CHAPTER 21

We had an uneventful daily process, which kept Emmi happy, as well as mentally and physically challenged. She ate and played on a regular schedule, which our lives were arranged to accommodate. Breaking her routine, however, posed challenges. When an unplanned event arose, it would throw us into a tizzy trying to figure out what to do with Emmi. She couldn't go to boarding or daycare. She was far too strong to play with most dogs and could hurt them with her wrestling moves. She had never learned proper puppy-play-behavior because she couldn't open her mouth and had to resort to body-slamming instead of puppy nips. Her feeding routine was cumbersome even for the most accomplished caregivers.

Emergencies were always a challenge. We were an hour away from home, returning from Izzy's ophthalmology appointment, when we found ourselves caught behind a fatal car accident resulting in standstill traffic. With nowhere to turn around or exit the freeway, we were stuck. Emmi had not been to the bathroom since we left the house early in the morning. We knew her bladder would be full and it was now approaching her dinnertime. I had ONE person I could call in these emergencies. Connie. The woman who originally picked up Emmi for Rottie Nation. Connie was a godsend. She lived minutes away and was always available at the drop of a hat. We were grateful for her friendship. Connie never worried that Emmi would protect the house and not let her in. They had an amazing bond. Even though Emmi was in the midst of faux motherhood with babies in her bed, she eagerly ran to Connie when she came through the door and tried to lead her to the bedroom where her "kids" were sleeping. She wanted to show off her new family.

December 26, 2014 was another one of those unforeseen events where we needed to lean on Connie. Ray and I were awake early, cleaning up from our celebration with friends the night prior. Ray was cooking breakfast and we were conversing about the fun we had on Christmas Day. A phone call changed everything.

"Hello."

"Is this Barbara Brunner, sister of Elizabeth?"

"Yes, how can I help you?" Thinking to myself, what has she done now? My sister had a history of substance abuse and despite many stints in rehab, was still addicted. I was sure she was in some sort of trouble again. Crashed another car. Perhaps something worse.

"Ma'am, would you please sit down. I am calling from the coroner's office." Her voice was deadpan. "Your sister was found dead this morning." There was no emotion in her voice. My heart skipped a beat or two. I am sure of it. I knew this day would probably come sooner than later, but it was still a shock. I had asked my sister many years prior to put an emergency contact note in her wallet containing my name and phone number. I was shocked that she actually had. That is how the coroner had known to call me so quickly. The rest of our immediate family had passed on. It was just my sister and myself remaining. It would have taken them days, perhaps weeks, to locate me without that note.

With nothing but white noise in my head, I handed the phone to Ray and began to cry. My sister had died alone, on Christmas Day or maybe Christmas Eve. The coroner wasn't sure. I had spoken to her on the afternoon of Christmas Eve. This phone call didn't seem real.

While we were celebrating Christmas, my sister overdosed and died. It was an accidental overdose. She was in the middle of wrapping presents for her small group of friends when she stood up, fell to the floor and died. Her friends were supposed to gather for a Christmas Eve dinner at her house. When she didn't answer the door, they called and got no answer. Her blinds were drawn and they assumed she had a headache and went to bed. Headaches for her were a code word for I just took a hit of drugs. When she was still not answering her phone the day after Christmas, one of her neighbors called the local police department to come do a Welfare Check.

That was when she was found.

Ray and I had to leave immediately to go to Pennsylvania. Izzy was easy. We could throw a bag of dog food and her medicine in the cooler and we would be ready to leave. Emmi was not so easy. It would have been almost impossible to take her with us. Her feeding preparation posed many complications for travel. Emmi and Izzy together in a car for days would have been challenging. To top it off, my sister had a cat named Finn. We could keep Izzy away from a cat but Emmi had never seen one, as far as we knew. It could have been chaotic. It would not have been fair to the dogs or to Ray who would have to manage the circus.

I called Connie. She had a houseful of family members staying with her for the holiday, but none-the-less, dropped everything to stay at our home with Emmi. She didn't even hesitate to say yes. She shuttled back and forth, cooking meals for her family and preparing meals for Emmi. Attending to Emmi's needs (thank goodness for a fenced yard) and became Emmi's playmate and sleeping buddy for a week. Connie brought her rescue Weimaraner, and Emmi's BFF, Bogie. They had a weeklong play-date. Emmi still had a bad habit of jumping up on people and it was a huge concern for me. Connie was spry, but she was breakable. I didn't want Emmi to get excited and knock her down by accident. I expressed my concern to Connie who told me point blank "Don't worry about it, I'll be just fine. Now go!"

Emmi had a gregarious nature offset by the strength of an elephant. While her intentions were always positive she could injure someone easily with her clumsiness and enthusiasm. It is something that with training and maturity she would outgrow, but we often warned visitors of her freight-train-without-brakes personality. She had grown so rapidly and her coordination was far from catching up to her size. Connie sat Emmi down and had a chat, telling her no jumping would be tolerated. Apparently Emmi understood and Connie remained upright for the entire week.

When we arrived home Emmi was happy to see us, but so balanced. She acted more like we had just gotten back from the store, not from a weeklong absence. Connie was an exceptional substitute momma.

While cleaning out my sister's home we were surprised at how well Izzy handled the presence of a cat. Poor Finn had been alone for at least a day with my sister's body. He was a loyal feline. The police asked a neighbor to take care of him until we arrived. We were not in my sister's home for more than five minutes when the cat was returned to us. Without a crate, without a litter box and without food. Ray and I are not cat people. We love all animals, but have no life skills when it comes to caring for a cat. Again, I appealed to my Facebook family for help. Within an hour we had Finn placed with a local rescue group who agreed to take him in, health issues unknown. We could not find any veterinary records of vaccinations or care that Finn had received. Pet Pantry Of Lancaster County gave him the medical treatment he needed and within a month, found Finn a forever home. They periodically updated me with news from his new mom and dad. He was in a lovely home with two senior citizens who doted on him. Animal rescuers are a special group of people. I am proud to count many among my friends, virtual and in-real-life. They have helped us through many difficult times.

Izzy's Perspective

CAR RIDE! I like car rides. Dad says we are going back to that Pennsylvania place. We've been there a lot in two years. My first trip was when mom's human dad died. Mom and I flew in an airplane. I like airplanes. I am a very good flier. Mom and I used to fly everywhere together. I got my wings from United Airlines. The pilot man told me I was better behaved than the screaming kids who were on that plane. I gave him a kiss on the nose when he pinned wings on my leash.

Dad and Morgan drove from Florida to Pennsylvania overnight. Morgan was too fat to fit on an airplane. It probably wouldn't have been able to take off with her on board. Ok, she wasn't really fat. That wasn't nice. She just wasn't trained to fly like me. I get to do all of the cool things because I'm special.

Morgan told me on their long car trip that they were really tired but she helped keep dad awake. And she got BURGERS! And French fries! See, I told you she was fat. I've never had burgers or fries, but she says they are delicious. I would break out in hives if I tried them. Morgan and I were very good on that trip. Morgan told me it was my job to behave and she was serious. No shenanigans. Mom was sad and we did our best to make her happy. Lots of people came to visit mom that week and I liked meeting them. My grandpa had a lot of nice friends.

The apartment smelled like my grandpa. I loved him so much. He taught me to do all kinds of stuff when I was little. He taught me to use the doggie door and to walk on a leash and to come and to sit and how to chase a ball. I found a needlepoint pillow on the sofa that smelled like him and mom let me keep it. She said HER mom made it a long time ago. I guess that would make that my grandma. I never met her, but I bet she was nice. I'll take very good care of that pillow. It's special. Like me!

My second trip to the Pennsylvania place was when Emmi had surgery. You know that story.

Now we have to go again. Road Trip! My mom's human sister died. Emmi can't go with us so I have mom and dad all to myself. Yay! Aunt Connie is going to babysit Emmi.

Emmi's a baby...Emmi's a baby... ooops. My terrier-isms are showing...

Why is Pennsylvania so cold? This makes three times being a terrier ice-pop. How do the people here survive? I know I wouldn't. I like it warm. If I were in charge, it would be warm everywhere!

Mom remembered to bring a coat for me and it helps to keep me from freezing to death. I have my princess bed in the car and mom keeps me covered with a blanket. There's white stuff on the ground called snow. It looks like sand, but it's not warm and toasty like sand. I don't like this snow stuff. It's cold on my feet. I heard mom say it was twenty degrees.

Dad seems to have the silly idea that I am going to pee in the snow. Wrong, dad. I'll hold it until the next millennium. I'm not peeing in snow. Never gonna happen. Brrr.

When we get to the place where my mom's sister lived, there's a CAT! I'm allergic - like that's a surprise to anyone? Cats make me sneeze and itch. Mom gives me some Benadryl and tells me to buck up and to be nice.

The cat is scared, so I'm going to be his friend. Dad says his name is Finn. I tell Finn not to worry. My mom and dad are the best in the world and they will find him new parents. I tell him I am sorry his human mom died. He says he was afraid when he was alone but now he will try to be brave. He is hungry and mom gives him some food she found in the pantry. Finn purrs a thank you. Mom says he is super cute and will get adopted fast. I hope so. The people at the cat adoption place are really nice to Finn. They get him a cage and a litter pan and food. I think he will be happy there until he finds his forever humans.

Emmi's Perspective

Mom got sad after the phone rang. I gave her lots of hugs to try to cheer her up. I don't understand why she is sad. Yesterday was my first real Christmas! We had so much fun. I got lots of presents. So did Izzy.

Mom says they are going to have to leave for a while but Aunt Connie is going to come and stay with me. I love my Aunt Connie. And Bogie is coming too! He's my bestest friend. He's a lot bigger than me. We can chase each other all around the yard and I don't have to worry about stepping on him. He gets tired some times. But after he sleeps, he plays with me again. Aunt Connie says he's old and I have to take it easy on him. But he's just so much fun!

Aunt Connie gives me a "talking to" right after mom leaves. She tells me she doesn't want me to jump up on her anymore. If I knock her down and she gets hurt who will feed me? I like to eat so I better be good and keep four on the floor.

I get to sleep with Bogie and Aunt Connie every night. I think we are having fun, but apparently I'm a little too enthusiastic. While Aunt Connie is trying to go to sleep I shove toys in her face. She has to put me in another room until I calm down. I can't help myself. Having a bedtime buddy is really nice. Bogie tells me to quiet down and go to sleep. I finally figure out if I want to sleep in the big bed, I better behave.

I hear mom and dad's car! They're home! Mom and dad, I missed you a lot but I had so much fun with Bogie and Aunt Connie! Wait a minute... Wait. A. Minute. The car smells like cat. Mom smells like cat. I know what cats are. They are the creatures with that scrumptious food I got after my first surgery. Mom cheated on me! Pfft. Oh well, I don't really care. I'm happy to see them and give them lots and lots of kisses. I told Izzy all about playing with Bogie and she told me about Finn. She never saw a cat before and he made her sneeze. A dog that is allergic to cats... That's funny.

CHAPTER 22

Emmi's second heat cycle in May 2015 offered less drama, but still inconvenience and frustration. Approximately two months later, we were faced with her second false pregnancy. We had hoped the one after her first heat cycle would be a one-off event, but apparently it is not uncommon for false pregnancies to recur. There's no explanation for it, but some female dogs are more prone to the hormonal fluctuations that cause the body to think it is pregnant, when in actuality it is not. Emmi was just an over-achiever in everything she did.

When Emmi's nesting instincts once again kicked in - which were natural but frankly a bit obsessive compulsive - one of her fans suggested we find her toy Rottweiler puppies to satisfy her maternal instinct. QUIET toys this time. Shortly after, we received an anonymous gift in the mail of two tiny plush Rottie toys about the size of newborn pups. Emmi got so excited when we presented them to her. She nuzzled them, bathed them regularly, and tucked them safely into her bed. It ended her compulsively crazy behavior almost immediately. She just needed babies to nurture and love. Since the real thing would never be a possibility, this was perfect for her. Her Facebook fans voted on names and soon they became Bogie and Bacall, or B&B for short.

Emmi pushed B&B all around the house. They had to be in the same room as her at all times or snuggled under a blanket on her bed. Emmi was as gentle as a ninety-four pound dog could be. Yes, if they were actual puppies they would have been smushed fairly quickly - Emmi's always been a tad bit clumsy - but she loved them and cared for them like any mother would. Or at least she tried. She bathed them so frequently that they soon became glopped with Emmi slobber, got very stinky, and needed washing. Emmi sat by the front-loading washer door watching B&B go round and round until they were placed into the dryer. It was reminiscent of what Cooper did when his stuffed talking elephant, Horton, was plopped into the washer so many years before. He would patiently wait for Horton to emerge first from the washer and then the dryer, never taking his eyes off the door until Horton was safely returned to his mouth. Emmi and Cooper always seemed to have an inexplicable connection. Emmi did not leave the laundry room until

B&B were snuggled back in her bed. She was such a loving and caring dog. If circumstances were different she may have made a wonderful mother.

After many long discussions with Dr. Sandy and other veterinary professionals, we made the decision to investigate the process of having Emmi spayed. Her heat cycles and false pregnancies were very difficult on her and she was losing a significant quality of life from the vast swings in her hormone levels. It would be a major and risky operation but we could not let her suffer through another heat cycle and false pregnancy if there was an alternative. Her chances of contracting Pyometra, a life threatening infection of the uterus, were increased the longer she stayed intact. We felt it safer to have a planned surgery rather than risk an emergency situation where she could lose her life. The surgeon Dr. Sandy consulted with and eventually chose for the operation had a team experienced in the tricky intubation procedure Emmi would need.

I group messaged her most ardent followers to apprise them of the upcoming events, asked for their good wishes, and above all asked for their confidentiality to not release any information to her Facebook Page until I felt she was out of danger. It gave me a group of devoted friends with whom I could share my fears and not frighten those who may not understand why we were going ahead with a risky procedure. We shared hundreds of messages over the next two days. It helped to have their love, no matter the outcome. I knew they would be my support team on Emmi's Facebook Page if things went terribly wrong.

The chosen surgeon devised a method where he threaded an intubation tube over a bronchoscope, used the camera to guide him down Emmi's throat to correctly place her breathing tube. He wanted to avoid a tracheostomy if at all possible since the scar tissue from her three previous procedures would be difficult to work around. Additionally it would leave her with a much more difficult operation if one were needed in a future emergency situation. An additional emergency veterinary surgeon and an anesthesiologist assisted him. The clinic where the procedure was to be performed was an emergency clinic with an ICU, so if anything went sideways, a crash cart team was standing by to assist. The surgeon explained the entire procedure to us in an hour-long conference the day prior to the operation. All precautions were being taken to ensure success. She would wear an oxygen mask and additional oxygen would be delivered to her through a tube running directly into her lung. The surgeon ensured there would be redundancy for every step of the procedure and we felt as confident as we could, considering the situation.

-The oxygen delivery system had a back up.

-If the intubation failed, she would already be prepped for a tracheostomy.

-A laparoscopic ovary removal surgery was planned. However once he had her open, if he had felt it necessary, he was prepared for a regular incision and a full hysterectomy.

He had a plan to address her opiate allergy and used a deep-tissue local anesthesia, followed by low dose opiates for 24 hours. His methodology was sound and he seemed very capable.

We sat on pins and needles all day. We dropped her off at 8:00 AM and surgery was to begin at 11:00 AM. Best-case scenario would have her in recovery by 1:00 PM. Worst case would have her finished by 3:00 PM.

As 2:00 PM came and went we knew things had not gone as smoothly as we had hoped, however, the surgeon explained it would be the first six minutes of surgery where the greatest danger laid. Without a phone call by noon we knew she had made it through the critical period.

At 4:00 PM we received the news that Emmi was out of surgery and doing well. A laparoscopic procedure had been attempted but because of her false pregnancy there were too many healthy blood vessels preparing her to be a mommy. The bleeding was too extensive, making a traditional incision necessary. Other than that, everything went off without a hitch. The best news of all was that she did not need a tracheostomy - the tube procedure had worked. We were so relieved and made arrangements to bring her home later that evening. She recovered quickly, returning to her happy, silly self.

CHAPTER 23

After her third surgery and the realization that Emmi's jaw would never function again, we were sad. I honestly think we mourned. She had been through so much and not gained anything other than her life. That had been spared but to what avail?

My pinky finger barely fits between her toothless gums at the front of her mouth. If there is any function of her jaw it can be measured in fractions of millimeters and that movement is from us forcing the movement, not her voluntarily moving the joint. She tries to open her mouth constantly and our hearts break watching her attempt to yawn.

We wipe slobber from her face constantly throughout the day. She needs Vaseline rubbed onto her tongue at night so it does not dry out. She can pull it back into her mouth to keep it wet, but chooses to let it hang out. Her remaining teeth get brushed after every meal. She has her own Waterpik and electric toothbrush to help prevent gingivitis where her molars clamp tightly shut. Every meal is the same liquefied slurry. She often gets food up her nose while eating and we worry that someday she might aspirate. But she is happy. She loves people. She has every right to hate the world for what she had been through, yet she does not. She wags her stubby tail even when we visit the veterinarian. She is a dog who puts a positive spin on her world.

Emmi has a guardian angel. I am certain of it. There is no other explanation for her ability to continually overcome the medical odds she has faced. I am not a particularly religious person but I was raised to believe in a higher being. Who or what that is, I do not know. But I firmly believe there has been someone or something watching over Emmi through all of the surgeries, infections and difficulties she's had in her short life. She is on this earth for a reason. I know that reason will reveal itself when the time is right. Perhaps she is here to become a therapy dog to help children overcome their fear of hospitals or disfigurement from similar surgeries. Maybe it is as simple as becoming a breed ambassador to show others that Rottweilers are not a dog to fear. Time will tell.

We understood when we adopted Emmi what the initial time requirements would be on us and how much attention it would take from us to get her healthy. We never allowed ourselves to believe that the surgeries might fail. We approached each procedure with hope. We expected there would be an end-date to the time drain when Emmi could be as self-sufficient as a dog can be. She remains a 24/7/365 undertaking. We don't get to take vacations because Emmi could never board in a doggie hotel. There would be too much risk. A small scuffle with another dog could result in disastrous consequences to her tongue. Even with the air conditioner at high speed, beaming sun through the car windows causes her to rapidly overheat eliminating even a short car ride to the store. A long day of shopping or appointments has to be planned well in advance so someone can be scheduled to swim with and safely exercise Emmi. And then there's the mealtime ritual - not for the faint of heart. She's a lot of work but we wouldn't have it any other way. Emmi has taught us so much about handling the challenges of life with a smile. She accepts her limitations and always finds a work-a-round. She is continually happy, positive, and never lets her specially-abled mouth cause her to miss a beat. We rarely see frustration. Only determination. And love. She returns what we give to her, tenfold.

In our initial discussion with each surgeon, we knew she would never be "normal," but expressed our desire for her to have enough function in her jaw to experience a good quality of life. We needed to be realistic. Emmi's happiness and ability to function in the world were paramount. If we had known what Emmi's future held, would we do it again? We were posed that question often in her first two years of life and honestly we don't know the answer. We doubt that she remembers being able to use her jaw normally. All she knows is that she has a loving home, eats on schedule and has two humans at her beck and call to amuse her.

When we throw our arms open and utter "Emmi come" she bounds to us, ears flapping, with a shine in her eyes. In those moments we know we did right by her. Emmi knows she is loved.

She. Is. Rottweiler.

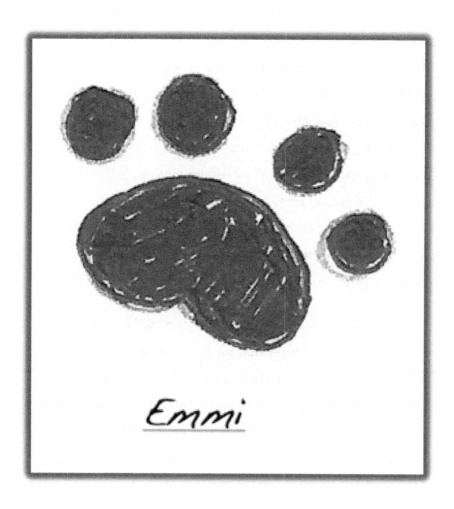

EPILOGUE

As I finish the final chapters of Emmi's book, I watch her playing in the pool, self-entertaining with her orange beach ball. She swims like an Olympic champion. I am occasionally soaked with pool water when she decides to come give me a kiss. Her blue Go-Frrr ball is slapped onto my lap with a playful look. "Come on Mom. Play with me! Let's have FUN!"

There is a distinct grinding noise coming from under my desk. It's Emmi, chewing on the handle of my file drawer. Chewing. I kid you not. The soft aluminum handles have the battle scars to prove it. I suspect there may be a sequel to Loving Emmi brewing. What will this amazing creature accomplish next...

ABOUT THE AUTHOR

Award winning author Barbara Boswell Brunner grew up in Lancaster County, Pennsylvania with her parents, sister and always a dog, or two or three. She graduated Summa Cum Laude from a small women's college in Bryn Mawr, Pennsylvania. Meeting her husband in Washington, DC, they continued together on a journey as self-proclaimed dog addicts. In the ensuing years, she founded three successful businesses in the Pacific Northwest and is a prolific fundraiser for breast cancer research. She and her husband are retired and now reside in Southwest Florida with two dogs and copious amounts of dog fur. She is currently working on indulging her serious flip-flop addiction.

If you would enjoy learning more details about the dogs that preceded Emmi and Izzy, they can be found in the first book of the Dog-Ma series, *Dog-Ma, The Zen Of Slobber*, available through Amazon or at DogmaTheBook.com. It is available in physical book format, as well as e-reader and audio formats.

Thank you for taking the time to read *Loving Emmi*. It has been a labor of love to complete. If you have enjoyed the book, reader reviews on Amazon are always appreciated.

Melissa Tan created the whimsical and original illustrations for *Loving Emmi*. They are wholly owned by Barbara Boswell Brunner and may not be copied or shared without express written permission. More of Melissa's work can be seen on her website; paintinks.by.melt.com.

Made in the USA
Middletown, DE
09 June 2023

32326066R00089